BOMBER COMMAND

FAILED TO RETURN II

Published in 2012 by Fighting High Ltd, 23 Hitchin Road,
Stotfold, Hitchin, Herts, SG5 4HP
www.fightinghigh.com

British Library Cataloguing-in-Publication data. A CIP record
for this title is available from the British Library.

ISBN 978 0 9562696 9 0

Designed by Michael Lindley www.truthstudio.co.uk.
Printed and bound by Toppan Printing Co. (SZ) Ltd.

BOMBER COMMAND
FAILED TO RETURN II

STEVE BOND, STEVE DARLOW, LINZEE DRUCE, SEAN FEAST
JULIAN EVAN-HART AND ANDREW MACDONALD

CONTENTS

52

20

76

108

96

68

42

8

84

30

60

INTRODUCTION

THE CASUALTY NUMBERS ARE SIMPLY STAGGERING – 55,573 AIRMEN WHO SERVED WITH RAF BOMBER COMMAND DURING THE SECOND WORLD WAR LOST THEIR LIVES IN THE FIGHT AGAINST NAZISM. A FURTHER 9,838 AIRMEN BECAME PRISONERS OF WAR AND 8,403 WERE WOUNDED IN ACTION. THESE EXTRAORDINARY AND UNPRECEDENTED LOSS STATISTICS ACCUMULATED AS THE RAF BOMBER CREWS PLAYED THEIR PART IN THE PROSECUTION OF ALLIED GRAND STRATEGY: DEFENDING THE BRITISH ISLES FROM INVASION, BLASTING THE ENEMY INDUSTRIAL INFRASTRUCTURE, SUPPORTING THE ALLIED LAND CAMPAIGNS, TARGETING THE ENEMY NAVY AND U-BOAT THREATS AND COUNTERING THE GERMAN V-WEAPON MENACE.

125,000
APPROXIMATE NUMBER OF AIRCREW WHO SERVED
WITH RAF BOMBER COMMAND DURING WWII

55,573
NUMBER OF AIRCREW WHO WERE KILLED WHILE
SERVING WITH RAF BOMBER COMMAND

IN THIS SECOND VOLUME DEDICATED TO BOMBER COMMAND AIRCREW WHO 'FAILED TO RETURN', FIGHTING HIGH PUBLISHING AGAIN BRINGS TOGETHER ACCLAIMED HISTORIANS TO TELL THE STORIES OF THOSE WHO BECAME CASUALTIES. ILLUSTRATED THROUGHOUT WITH COLOUR AND BLACK-AND-WHITE PHOTOGRAPHS, THE VAST MAJORITY PREVIOUSLY UNPUBLISHED, *BOMBER COMMAND: FAILED TO RETURN II* CONTINUES TO ENSURE THAT THE MEMORY OF THE BOMBER BOYS, WHO SACRIFICED ALL, IS KEPT ALIVE.

'LEST WE FORGET.'

8,403
NUMBER OF AIRCREW WHO WERE WOUNDED
WHILE SERVING WITH RAF BOMBER COMMAND

9,838
NUMBER OF AIRCREW WHO BECAME PRISONERS
OF WAR

CHAPTER ONE

BLENHEIM DOWN

JULIAN EVAN-HART

IN A PARTICULARLY REMOTE AREA AMONG THE ISOLATED MATURE CONIFERS IN THE WOODED REGION OF WOUDENBERGSEWEG, WHICH IS NEAR ZEIST IN HOLLAND, THERE IS A PLACE WHERE, IF ONE LOOKS VERY CAREFULLY, A FEW SMALL SCATTERED TWISTED PIECES OF METAL CAN BE SEEN.

THE CASUAL OBSERVER would perhaps never notice these small often moss-covered items, and indeed many people since the Second World War, walking past, have failed to take an interest. Even if the pieces are noticed, they would probably be discounted as items of corroding modern junk left behind by some careless campers a few decades back and consequently not even given a second thought. However, to the trained and experienced eye, such things are very different. There are a few people in recent years who have dedicated much of their lives to looking for just such small seemingly insignificant scraps of metal. Most people walk on by, but just recently several have actually stopped and contemplated and have then turned on their metal detectors hoping for that clear or faint signal in their headphones – a signal that will reveal buried artefacts that are not visible to the keen roving eye. Superb standards of research, awareness and sharp eyesight will all help, but usually it is the metal detector that finally clinches the deal and confirms

that what has been searched for has now finally been found. In 2011 it was just such a small group of people who stood here, and indeed contemplated the scene, before conducting a metal-detecting survey of the surrounding area. Their dedicated research and time spent locating eye-witnesses had finally brought them their reward: a handful of old twisted and corroded aluminium pieces.

This desolate area in a section of coniferous woodland near Zeist is exactly where, some seventy years ago, an RAF Bristol Blenheim aircraft came crashing to earth. For all air crashes, there is usually a story to tell, a story that is likely to contain the various elements of bravery, pain, death, survival and sheer damned good luck – or perhaps, on occasion, the lack of it. To uncover and reveal such elements often involves in-depth research, and even this sometimes draws a complete blank or may leave extensive gaps of knowledge. However, when researching such incidents, such gaps in knowledge, although very frustrating, are not the main issue for

Below On a cold winters day, Edwin van Engelen stands on the very spot where the Blenheim crashed on 27 June 1940. *(Stichting Legerplaats Soesterberg 1939–1945)*

the majority of those concerned. In the incident we are about to review, there are no known photographs of any of the airmen involved here. No doubt photographs remain somewhere, perhaps captured in group shots or on the dusty shelves of a junk shop. Sometimes it is distant relatives who are able to provide photographs, finally putting a face to a long-researched individual or a complete crew. In the author's experience, these photographs usually appear after the research has been published, and such is fate. Although it would be fascinating to see what these individuals looked like, the lack of images nonetheless does not detract from the importance of telling their story. The main issue is that artefacts deriving from such incidents are not just archaeologically revealing, they can actually form items of memorial. Many such artefacts are carefully cleaned, conserved and displayed in collections all over Europe: tangible memorials – albeit rather inadequate ones – to the bravery of such young men.

Of course, nothing can ever make up for what they and their families went through in the final

continually and visually expressed by just such torn shredded fragments of metal. With the assistance of many people I feel very honoured and highly privileged, therefore, to be able to present and tell the final story of Blenheim R3731 and her crew. Wherever possible, the account remains factual, but some elements have out of necessity been left to the creativity of the author.

Early on the morning of Thursday, 27 June 1940, the ground crew had bustled around the parked Blenheim MkIVs. The sounds of their shouts, muffled comments and clanking spanners were carried across the airfield on the slight breeze. The sun rose and shone brightly over RAF Watton airfield that morning. Small flurries of dust and dry grass fragments raced across the concrete surface of the runways. These Blenheims, many of which had already seen extensive combat in Europe, were from No. 82 Squadron, which formed part of No. 2 Group Bomber Command. They had already played a very prolific part in the action against the enemy. The extreme level of their combat experience and perhaps the shortfall of the Bristol

Missions and losses of No. 82 Squadron 10 May 1940–30 June 1940

Not all operations are listed here; however, those with fatal losses are.

14 May 1940	Breda, NL	—
17 May 1940	Gembloux, B.	12 planes lost; 8 KIA, 13 MIA, 3 POW
22 May 1940	Hesdin, F.	1 plane lost, 3 KIA
7 June 1940	Reconnaissance, F.	1 plane lost
8 June 1940	Abbeville, F.	2 planes lost, 2 KIA, 2 POW
8 June 1940	Battle Area, F.	1 plane lost, 1 KIA, 2 POW
9 June 1940	?, UK	1 KIA or DOW
13 June 1940	Forêt de Gault, F.	3 planes lost, 3 KIA, 1 MIA, 2 POW
25 June 1940	Training, UK	1 plane lost, 1 KIA
27 June 1940	NW Germany	1 plane lost, 2 KIA, 1 POW (*crashed in NL*)
2 July 1940	Dortmund-Ems Canal, D	1 plane lost, 3 KIA (*crashed in NL*)

moments of life or for decades afterwards. If it was not for the efforts of people like Edwin van Engelen, as in this case, then perhaps the experiences of these young airmen and of others in thousands of similar incidents would be locked away in dry musty-smelling documentary records, only ever being revealed via specific research. Their exploits and indeed sometimes their very short lives can be

Blenheim in such combat had already been seriously highlighted.

On 17 May 1940 twelve Blenheims from No. 82 'United Provinces' Squadron had taken off to attack German troop concentrations at Gembloux in Belgium. Initially they had been promised fighter escort from Hurricanes, but these fighters had been intercepted earlier, which delayed them. So the

Blenheims had proceeded unescorted, to be attacked by fifteen Messerschmitt Bf109s. Within minutes eleven Blenheims had been shot down, and the single damaged survivor, coded UX-W, had just managed to limp back to base, only to be written off, because of the extensive damage it had received. It was only due to the sheer perseverance and dedication of its commanding officer, the Earl of Brandon, that within forty-eight hours No. 82 Squadron was re-equipped and able to fight again. The earl's persistence would be tested in the future, when, on 13 August 1940, once again No. 82 Squadron suffered very serious losses. A brief glimpse at some of No. 82 Squadron's missions and losses confirms that, although one could say that the Squadron was certainly experienced in combat, it most definitely could not be considered to be lucky.

Back at Watton airfield on 27 June 1940, the crews had been briefed and informed that the operations for the day would involve the German city of Hanover and reconnaissance runs over the French coast. In total the ground crews had prepared twenty-four aircraft: twelve were going to Germany and twelve to France. As each three-man crew clambered aboard their aircraft, the surrounding countryside reverberated to the roar of forty-eight 905-horsepower Bristol Mercury XV radial engines. As each crew took off, they could see the little village of Griston to the right. Some might even have noticed the darker 'fairy rings' in the grass of the locally famous mushroom meadows.

Having taken off, the aircraft divided into their two respective groups. We will now follow the twelve that had been selected for the German target of Hanover. This sizeable German city on the River Leine in Lower Saxony offered some very important oil-industry-based targets. One of these twelve aircraft was Blenheim MkIV, coded UX-Y No. R3731. On board that day were Pilot Officer

Left Fire damaged and corroded drum of bullets from a Vickers K machine gun. The bullet casings are exploded examples recovered from the crash site and placed in situ. *(Stichting Legerplaats Soesterberg 1939–1945)*

Arthur A. Stanley, who was the observer, Pilot Officer Ralph A. Percy, the pilot, and Sergeant Andrew M. Clark, the wireless operator/air gunner. Deteriorating weather conditions meant that, of the twelve planes attacking, only six managed to drop their loads of four 250lb bombs. Despite this, several oil installations received direct hits and burst into flames, producing huge columns of black smoke. When weather deterioration dictated, it seems that, on occasion, pilots would decide to investigate other potential targets. Sometimes these targets would be officially scheduled and sanctioned and sometimes they were purely opportunistic. A great favourite for failed German target operations was to locate and attack the airfields in Occupied Holland. This appeared to be the plan associated with what took place on this day. For, at around 1615 hours, three of No. 82 Squadron's Blenheims suddenly appeared over Soesterberg airfield and began to circle round at a height of 1,000 metres in the partly cloudy skies. Already alerted to the activity overhead, far down below them the pilots of the third Staffel of Jagdgeschwader 21, under

the command of Geschwader Kommodor Martin Metting, were taking off in their Messerschmitt Bf109 E-1s. Gaining altitude quickly, they soon engaged the much slower Blenheims, and individual combats began to form. The Blenheims were scattered and one of them, attempting to gain altitude, dropped its four bombs very near to a German Army encampment known as 'Dumoulin Kazerne'. 3/JG 21, which had been at Soesterberg only since 23 June 1940, were anxious to get to grips with the increasing RAF raiders in their area, and among the pilots that day was their very experienced 26-year-old Staffel Kapitan Oberleutnant Georg Schneider. Schneider had already shot down six aircraft in this war, but, unknown to anyone at this stage, was a matter of minutes away from increasing this score to seven.

The clouded skies seemed to be full of wheeling and jinking aircraft; Schneider well knew that in such situations an opportunity could be presented and then denied in just a split second. As always he was determined to increase his tally, and initially both fate and luck chose to enhance this ambition and were firmly on his side. He increased his speed

Right Anomalies of war. One of the aluminium manufacturers specification plates from the Blenheim can be seen to be Daimler. The irony could not be more pronounced. *(Stichting Legerplaats Soesterberg 1939–1945)*

Left Small copper alloy specification plate. *(Stichting Legerplaats Soesterberg 1939–1945)*

and was some distance out in front of his colleagues, which included Feldwebel Paul Pausinger, when one of the RAF Blenheims suddenly crossed over in front of him. Schneider banked and followed. Throttling back so as not to overshoot the target, Schneider watched the twin-engine RAF aircraft increase in size through the Revi gun sight. It was now exactly 1620 hours and the young Luftwaffe ace contained within his Me109 E-1 continued to watch with intent as the Blenheim now started to make mild evasive manœuvres. He followed, then his target levelled out and made a dash for it, but Schneider was firmly behind and followed with sheer determination. Grasping the control column of his Messerschmitt 109, he deftly flicked up the gun cover and now began gently to apply pressure to both gun buttons with his thumb and forefinger. With a sharpshooter's mind, he knew the situation had to be just right and he would know precisely when that was. He was flying behind the Blenheim just slightly off to port when he finally squeezed and fully depressed both buttons. Above the roar of the Messerschmitt's Daimler Benz 601 engine, Schneider could clearly hear the staccato rhythm of the four MG17 machine guns. He saw the four spiralling smoky threads of tracer heading through the sky towards his target and could just smell the sharp acrid smell of explosive. In just over a single second later the Blenheim's tail section was spattered with brilliant white flashes and puffs of creamy smoke. The rear landing wheel was hit and its rubber tyre violently burst apart, as other bullets began to strike along the fuselage heading towards the dorsal turret. Because of the angle of impact, many rounds created long gouges of ripped metal surrounded by patches of splintered paint as they ripped through the airframe.

Moments previously the dorsal turret gunner of the Blenheim, Sergeant Andrew M. Clark, had seen the sky full of enemy fighters and hoped against all odds that they would stay away. He watched as several broke away and began to follow his Blenheim. One appeared to be gaining on them much faster than the others. Meanwhile, some distance away he had noticed some tracer rounds whizzing past, but they did not come from the aircraft pursuing them. Clark delayed opening fire because he wanted to make every round count; he knew the shortcomings of the Blenheim against a seriously determined single-engine fighter. No way could they outrun such a combat; it was left to the luck and guile of his experienced pilot, Ralph Percy. Despite this he also wondered just how effective his single Vickers K gun would be. As Clark watched, the engine cowling and wing sections of their pursuer began to flash and sparkle. A fraction before the enemy plane's bullets began to impact on the Blenheim, Clark returned fire, just as he saw his attacker banking to port. It was a burst of fire that probably took no longer than two seconds. The Messerschmitt's 7.92mm rounds now began to spatter into the Blenheim's tail section and along the fuselage, up along and into the dorsal turret. The Perspex of the turret began to shatter, as bullets punched neat circular frosty-edged holes or complete triangular sections out of it, several thumping into the body of the young gunner. The 22-year-old Andrew Clark had been killed instantly.

The impacting rounds continued up along the fuselage into the cockpit, also taking the life of Pilot Officer Ralph Arthur Percy, the pilot. Andrew Clark never saw the effects of his valiant burst of fire. Even had he lived, the attacking Messerschmitt would anyway soon have been obscured from his vision by the wind-blasted flames and grey-brown smoke now issuing from both of the Blenheim's engines. Thick smoke and flames were now streaking past the battered turret, leaving a long dark very visible trail in the overcast sky. The Blenheim was in severe trouble, and at low altitude the chances of bailing out were becoming virtually non-existent.

As Schneider had banked to port, his aircraft too started to receive strikes from the rounds fired by the Blenheim's dorsal gunner. Several of these punched into the thin-side cockpit Perspex of the Messerschmitt, causing severe head wounds to its pilot. With no conscious pilot, the Me109 also fell away and started to dive earthwards. It finally smashed into the ground 5 kilometres south-west of Soesterberg. Never having regained consciousness, Georg Schneider had been unable to bail out and had plummeted with his plane.

The combat had been watched by several people on the ground, mainly forestry and plantation workers, some of whom now began to run to where they anticipated the smoking British plane would come down. It descended at considerable speed but at a fairly shallow angle. At this point the only

survivor from this duel made his bid for freedom. Pilot Officer Stanley bailed out from the stricken aircraft only a few hundred metres from the ground. He sustained several cuts and bruises but was otherwise in reasonable shape. As his parachute canopy billowed open with a jolt, he watched as his Blenheim fell further. At over 250mph, it clipped the first tips of the uppermost branches of some conifers in woodland at Woudenbergseweg near Austerlitz. Flocks of startled woodpigeons burst from out of the treetops and scattered over the top of the wood. The Blenheim's propeller blades were now trimming away small green clumps of the needle-like foliage.

As the bomber descended through the woodland canopy, the branches and trunks increased in size and became more resistant. First the aircraft's wingtips were torn off and folded up, and then the pine tree fronds slapped against the Perspex-clad frontal section, which moments later was smashed and impacted by tree trunks. The aircraft then began to disintegrate as thicker trees divided up its structure. The huge engines, still under power, splintered the tree trunks as they were hurled forwards, torn from their mountings. The mid-fuselage broke aft of the wing section, and the tail unit detached and broke up among the trees. The mid-section of the fuselage crumpled up and catapulted the remains of the turret containing the dead gunner near to the remains of the cockpit. The engines crashed through the trees and hit the ground, sending up great spurts of the dark pine-needle-rich sandy soil as they bounced across the woodland floor. Each engine had screamed as its propeller blades had buckled and distorted and then the crank shafts had folded. Finely engineered components came to an instant stop of grinding metal and shearing of gear cog teeth as the cylinder pots broke away in a violent flurry of hot oil and woodland soil. The main bulk of the fuselage and wing root area had disintegrated into hundreds of pieces of contorted metal and caught fire as the fuel tanks had ruptured. The fire started to ignite the flammable sap of some nearby conifer trees.

As the fire took hold, the crackling of the burning pine trees was punctuated by exploding .303 bullets from the wreckage. A few hundred metres away, Sergeant Stanley also crashed through

Right
Small brass union clearly showing the Air Ministry and quality acceptance stamps. *(Stichting Legerplaats Soesterberg 1939–1945)*

the tops of the pine trees and finally hit the ground. Soon a large billowing column of dirty brown and white smoke began to rise above the woodland. Stanley knew that, even if people had not seen the Blenheim crash, they would certainly see this, so he needed to get away. He would not have noticed that over a kilometre away was another far smaller column of grey-white smoke that was emanating from yet another crashed aircraft, the Messerschmitt Bf109 of Georg Schneider. Twenty-six-year-old Georg Schneider had failed to bail out of the Messerschmitt. The diary of JG21 mentions that no reason could be established for this failure. Literally interpreted, this could mean that his body was badly damaged or consumed by fire, rendering any medical assessment of previous sustained injuries impossible. His body was recovered from the debris that had once been his Me109 and he was buried the very next day with full military honours.

Stanley was lucky. People had not only seen the dogfight above; they had seen him bale out. But he was fortunate because they were friendly Dutch forest workers and lumberjacks. Quickly locating the wounded British airman, they hustled him into a nearby wooden shack. It was not long until the Germans were scouring the area, and the foresters then suggested to Stanley that he depart and hide deeper in the woods. Later on two of the workers re-located Stanley and then took him to Austerlitz. Behind him in the wood lay the smashed and burning remains of his Blenheim. This was a nerve-wracking trip, as on the way they were stopped by a German officer. He asked the group if they 'had seen a British pilot', to which the two Dutchmen replied they had not, while Stanley just kept quiet. After a while the German officer allowed them to carry on with their journey. Previously two of their colleagues had grabbed all his flying clothing and parachute and buried them in the woodland. Eventually one of the forest workers took Stanley back to his house and dressed his wounds. He also gave him some old clothes and a small amount of money. The Dutchman then walked with him about a kilometre along the road to Utrecht and then departed. From here, however, Stanley's luck expired, and he was taken prisoner while on board a train shortly afterwards.

He would go on to spend his wartime captivity as Prisoner No. 84 in Camps L1, L6 and No. 357. However, the story does not end here. The Germans rightly assumed that, to get so far, Stanley must have been assisted and that the forest workers could be the only ones to have instigated this. In total, six civilians had assisted Stanley, and they were soon arrested. On 25 July 1940 the case against them was presented at the Deutsches Kriegsmarine court in Utrecht. Incredibly, the session lasted for over six hours, but the final sentence, which could probably have been assumed much earlier, was one of the death sentence for all parties. However, amazingly it was not finalized or carried out. Fortunately, the court President had very strong Dutch connections. Consequently, the prime suspect received just three years in prison. Four others were each sentenced to two years in prison and the sixth was acquitted because of lack of evidence. They were lucky. In the later stages of the war civilians – indeed anyone assisting Allied airmen in such circumstances – would be shot. Days later the German authorities allowed photographers from the Dutch press to attend the crash scene. Without doubt this was not freedom of the press but more likely a useful exercise for its propaganda value. The German soldiers then began clearing up the larger sections of airframe, engines and propeller blades. The bodies of both RAF airmen were laid to rest in the cemetery at Gemeentelijke begraafplaats Zeist/Woudenbergseweg 46 (just 800 metres from the crash site).

Details of the two RAF crewmembers killed.

Clark, Andrew Milne

Nationality:	United Kingdom
Rank:	Sergeant (W.Op./Air Gnr.)
Unit:	82 Sqdn.
Age:	22
Date of Death:	27 June 1940
Service No:	749331

Additional information: Son of George and Maggie M. Milne Clark of Elgin, Morayshire. Grave/Memorial Reference: Grave 1106.

Percy, Ralph Arthur

Nationality:	United Kingdom
Rank:	Pilot Officer (Pilot)
Unit:	82 Sqdn.
Age:	21
Date of Death:	27 June 1940
Service No:	42640

Additional information: Son of Malcolm Boyer and Alice Mary Percy, of Croydon, Surrey Grave/Memorial Reference: Grave 1105.

Post-war research has, of course, thrown up several anomalies and considerations connected with this incident.

1. During an interview conducted in 1990, Stanley apparently recalled that 'he was surprised that the Me109 had been shot down at all, since the Blenheim's gunner had been killed in the first burst of machine gun fire'. Stanley also stated that the source for his replacement clothing was not the Dutch forest worker but in fact a local scarecrow. There may be some factual essence in this. If the Dutch foresters had taken him to the wooden shack and removed his RAF uniform and other gear, then it would not have left him with much clothing. Therefore in this state one might consider that the German officer who met them later in the woods might well have been suspicious of Stanley's appearance. So, until he received better-quality replacement clothes at the forester's house in Austerlitz, there is every possibility that he was indeed temporarily dressed in clothing borrowed in some urgency from a local scarecrow.

2. Furthermore, Georg Schneider's Me109 is listed as crashing south of Soesterberg at 1635 hours, at exactly the same time a No. 235 Squadron Blenheim IV L9447 also came down in the same area. Could the two events have become inextricably confused and are now somehow connected? This has indeed been considered to be the case for many years. However, Richard de Mos interviewed an eyewitness who specifically stated that he had watched this dogfight, with both planes firing at each other, and they had both crashed at the same time. This eyewitness also stated that the Blenheim involved in this combat was the one that fell in Woudenbergseweg wood at the point where the crash site has been located, which has been identified beyond doubt as that of R3731.

3. More confusion is apparent concerning Georg Schneider's first point of interment. Some records state that he was buried the very next day with full military honours at Grebbeberg, while other records claim he was first interred at Friedhof Soesterberg. Today, some seventy years later, one thing is certain: his remains now rest peacefully in the German cemetery at Ysselsteyn, Limburg. Recent consultation with documentary evidence (the Luftwaffe Verlust Meldung) has clarified that Schneider was in fact first interred at Friedhof Soesterberg, which, of course, does seem logical. He was then later reburied at Ysselsteyn. (Thanks go to local historian H. Wilson from Bilthoven.)

4. Allowing for the combat time of 1620 and even giving a generous 30 seconds for it all to be over, it does seem remarkable that Georg Schneider's Me109 took another 14.5 minutes to come to earth – officially that is – unless, of course, there were other Me109 incidents in the area that may have been confused both during and since the war. As Richard rightly pointed out, this time difference could also simply be down to the inaccuracies of wartime-created documents.

5. Some records indicate that the cause of the crash of Blenheim IV R3731 is 'Unknown'.

....

Seventy years later, four local aviation historians and researchers (Chris de Boer, Richard de Mos, Erwin Rust and Edwin van Engelen) set up a group called Stichting Legerplaats Soesterberg 1939–1945, dedicated to studying all military activities in these years, including aviation, the mobilization of Dutch forces, the German Occupation and Canadian/British military activity during the Liberation. The members of the group had previously each been conducting independent research since the 1980s, but in 2010 they all

decided to combine all their work. Their aim is to preserve the local history associated with 1939–1945 'so that it may never be forgotten'. One day in February Chris and Edwin were metal detecting in the wood at Woudenbergseweg looking for evidence of military activity in this area of the forest. Rumours had persisted that a British aircraft had crashed somewhere in the locality in 1940. Ironically, it was a local forester who finally came to their aid. He had been watching them metal detecting and finally decided to walk over and see what it was they were trying to find. The two men explained in some detail that they were looking for evidence of Dutch, German and Canadian military presence in the area. The man listened enthralled with all the details and then smiled as he revealed he knew of something that might interest them. He explained that there was a place in the wood where an RAF aeroplane had crashed during the war. Moreover the forester revealed he had been told by his father that the plane was a British Blenheim! This was excellent news. Stichting Legerplaats Soesterberg 1939–1945 had searched for this crash site several times previously with no success. Even better, the forester

explained that his father, while a small boy aged 12, had been involved in helping the only survivor to escape. There was not enough time to show the group the crash site on the day of the first meeting, but they quickly arranged to have a further meeting.

Within a matter of minutes of the second meeting with the forester, what had already taken several years of research seemed finally to be in their grasp. They were shown the alleged site of the crash deep in the woodland and eagerly switched on their metal detectors. Shortly afterwards small fragments of much corroded airframe began to be found. The coniferous trees had made the already acidic sandy soil even more so, and consequently much of the metal was just blue-white powdery oxide. But this did not put the research group off at all and, as they searched, more fragments were revealed, some of which were not so badly corroded. The four members of the group returned many times and made some remarkable discoveries. After a while they noticed that the crash site had about ten to fifteen holes in which much wreckage had been dumped. The foresters confirmed there had never before been anybody researching or digging

the site. So they concluded that these holes had most likely been excavated by German soldiers to bury all the smaller pieces deemed not worthy of recovery. Incredibly, from nearby one of these holes was excavated an empty ammunition drum from a Vickers K machine gun. Several fired .303 bullet casings were also located among many others that had exploded in the heat. Some of these casings were still in heavily corroded steel links. Early MkIV Blenheims were very undergunned, having a single Browning .303 link-fed gun in the port wing and a single Vickers K gun in the dorsal turret. So it would seem that the group have found archaeological evidence for both of these guns. Many manufacturers' labels were unearthed, along with flying helmet poppers (still fastened) and many Air Ministry-stamped components. A particularly poignant find was a tiny section of Perspex ruler which had once been part of Pilot Officer Stanley's navigational kit.

An interesting discovery of a British 250lb bomb was made some years back to the south of the area, where the previous German Army camp at 'Dumoulin Kazerne' had been positioned. The bomb was located in the area where an eyewitness had seen one of the Blenheims release its bombs on 27 June 1940. Like Edwin and his fellow group members, the author believes that this recently located bomb was indeed one of the four bombs dropped by a fleeing No. 82 Squadron Blenheim on 27 June 1940. Apparently this particular area was not subject to much bombing during the war. Moreover, the Blenheim in question was at very low altitude when it dropped its load, and therefore it is quite possible that one of its bombs did not detonate.

They went on to find fragments of shattered engine casing, manufacturers' labels and many other fascinating artefacts. All of these are currently being restored and will form part of the group's many exhibitions. At the time of writing, the exact whereabouts of Georg Schneider's Messerschmitt Bf109 crash site are not known. Because of the terrain and sparse rural nature of the area, local eyewitnesses were few in 1940 and are even fewer today. However Edwin van Engelen assures me that he and the rest of the group are confident that they are going to locate it.

The telling of this account, as previously stated, does indeed throw up some curious anomalies. However, as regards the identification of Blenheim R3731 and its exact crash site, this is now confirmed. What has not always been so certain is the question of who really did shoot down Georg Schneider. This can be problematic, as researchers like to be as historically accurate as possible. I believe that here, with the efforts of Stichting Legerplaats Soesterberg 1939–1945, this issue has been solved. History, rumour and fate have selected a young 22-year-old man, the son of George and Maggie Clark from Elgin in Morayshire, to be accredited with this action, and the author sees no factual reason or any evidence now remaining to attempt to remove this credit from its current association with Sergeant Andrew Milne Clark. Hopefully, this chapter will serve, alongside the work of Stichting Legerplaats Soesterberg 1939–1945, as a dedicational memorial to all those involved. ●

Left A British 250lb bomb unearthed nearby, in the vicinity of a German Army camp named 'Dumoulin Kazerne'. It was almost certainly dropped by one of the fleeing No. 82 Squadron Blenheims on 27 June 1940. *(Raimondo Bogaars)*

CHAPTER TWO

TAKING ON THE BEAST

STEVE DARLOW

BRITISH PRIME MINISTER WINSTON CHURCHILL WAS KEEN TO SINK THE 'BEAST' – THE NAME HE GAVE TO THE GERMAN BATTLESHIP *TIRPITZ*. HE WANTED THE THREAT ERADICATED, THEREBY REDUCING THE MENACE TO ALLIED SHIPPING IN THE NORTH SEA AND ATLANTIC AND FREEING UP THE ROYAL NAVY FOR OTHER THEATRES OF OPERATIONS. THE *TIRPITZ* HAD BEEN DECLARED READY FOR OPERATIONS IN JANUARY 1942 AND HAD MOVED TO NORWAY, FROM WHERE SHE ENDANGERED ALLIED CONVOYS. SKULKING AMID THE NORWEGIAN FJORDS, THE TIRPITZ SIMPLY HAD TO BE FOUND AND SHE HAD TO BE DESTROYED. AT THE END OF MARCH AND INTO APRIL 1942, BOMBER COMMAND WAS CALLED ON TO SINK THE 'BEAST'. A YOUNG SCOTSMAN, A TELEGRAM BOY AT THE START OF THE WAR, WOULD BE PART OF THE ATTACKING FORCE – AND 'FAILED TO RETURN'.

JOHN 'JOCK' MORRISON was born on 19 December 1921 in Woodside, Aberdeen, and at the age of 4 moved to nearby Bucksburn. He left school at 14 and became a local telegram boy, getting to know virtually everyone who lived in the nearby villages, including many of the local lads who were a couple of years older than Jock and who were Territorials in the Gordon Highlanders. 'They were all taken to France and all finished up at St Valéry-en-Caux in June 1940, ending up as prisoners of war'.

Three months after his eighteenth birthday, Jock volunteered for the Royal Air Force.

My dad was in the First World War and I had heard one or two stories, although not from him. He was badly wounded – his right shoulder was more or less blown away. And they all had bayonets and used to stick them into one another, so I thought I'm not having that. The Navy? There's far too much water. So I volunteered for the RAF, AC2 General Duties, the lowest of the low.

Jock was called up in June 1940 and joined thousands of other novices in Blackpool. They were marched through the town and allocated a boarding house. 'A lot of the landladies were not happy, because they were only getting the basic allowance from the RAF.' Jock shared his billet with around eighteen other Scotsmen, and the first morning porridge was served. 'There was sugar on the damn stuff. Aargh – take it away. You don't take sugar with porridge.'

After a couple of months of delights such as 'square bashing', Jock and his colleagues were called into a local cinema and the officers asked who would like to be wireless operators. 'I just sat there.' But the two lads either side of Jock stood up and pulled him up. 'So I "volunteered" to be a wireless operator.' A few weeks later Jock found himself in a similar position. 'They asked who would like to be rear gunners and the same two were sitting next to me and they pulled me up and that's how I "volunteered" to be an air gunner.'

Jock carried out his wireless training at RAF Yatesbury until November 1940, at one time having a 48-hour pass and travelling to London. 'I remember walking down Park Lane at night and the guns were going and the air raid sirens were going.' Jock carried out his gunnery training at RAF West Freugh, near Stranraer, finishing at the end of January 1941, and was then given a choice of stations, choosing RAF Dyce, near Aberdeen. 'I was living at home.' But after a short period there, when 'nobody wanted anything to do with us', Jock was sent to RAF Kinloss and an Operational Training Unit. Training continued on an individual basis, and Jock was eventually posted to RAF Middleton St George in June 1941, to fly Armstrong-Whitworth Whitleys, carrying out his first operation on 26/27 June with No. 78 Squadron. 'In those days we weren't all crewed up – not set crews like later in the war. I don't think I ever flew with the same pilot twice.' Jock recalls his feelings of finding out he was to fly his first operational sortie.

Left Sergeant Jock Morrison, wireless operator/air gunner, No. 35 Squadron. *(John Morrison)*

Right Jock Morrison,
seated second
from the left, at
Operational Training
Unit RAF Kinloss,
May 1941.
(John Morrison)

You were thankful that your name was on the board. Thankful that at long last you were going to do what you had been trained to do. We were all called into the crew room and names were up on the board. You were now going to be one of the squadron. You were going to be one of the boys.

I did my first three operations as 2nd wireless operator, so two as rear gunner and the third one as 1st wireless operator – you were being 'screened', a case of making sure you were up for it.

The first raid I ever did was to Cologne of all places and the skipper was asking everyone how they were. The skipper said 'You alright at the back there Jock?' I said, 'Yes Skip.' He said, 'Can you see anything?' I replied, 'Yep. What the hell are all these black puffs of smoke that keep following us?' 'Jesus Christ!' and he dived about 2,000 feet.

That night, of the thirty-two Vickers Wellingtons and nineteen Whitleys sent to Cologne, only seven aircraft reported carrying out an attack. Jock's Whitley was one of those that encountered the severe electrical storms. They could not locate the target, and brought the bombs back. Three nights later Jock was in the rear turret of one of 106 aircraft sent to attack Bremen. His task: 'To be awake at all times, eyes scanning, watching everything in your vision, making sure nothing was moving.' Seven aircraft failed to return, including a No. 78 Squadron Whitley with a total loss of life.

Throughout the summer months of 1941 further members of No. 78 Squadron 'failed to return'. 'You kept on seeing people there one day and they wouldn't be there the next. You didn't forget about it. You couldn't forget. But you didn't worry about it. It was a strange life.' While at Middleton St George, Jock witnessed a dreadful accident. 'A terrible day. We were sitting outside the crew room, just passing time. An aircraft was coming in to land, which had been practising with a fighter. They hit one another and down they came – no survivors.'

One day in September 1941, with eight operations under his belt, Jock was doing circuits and bumps, 'and this young pilot, it wasn't his fault, took 6 attempts to land the Whitley'.

The next morning I went in to the flight commander's office and said, 'I don't want to fly with him again!' 'You don't want to fly Morrison?'

Left Jock Morrison, wireless operator/ air gunner. *(John Morrison)*

I was asked. 'No, no. I just don't want to fly with him.' The flight commander asked, 'Are you going on leave?' and I said yes. When I came back after a fortnight's leave I was posted to No. 51 Squadron.

Jock flew three operations with No. 51 Squadron and then a request went out for volunteers to transfer to fly the new Handley Page Halifaxes with either No. 35 Squadron at RAF Linton-on-Ouse or No. 76 Squadron at RAF Middleton St George. When at RAF Middleton St George Jock had been courting his future wife, Margery, so he volunteered for the station that would facilitate further romance. But 'I got Linton-on-Ouse – such is life!'

Jock had met Margery at a church hall dance in Darlington. The wedding was arranged for 21 February 1942, a very wintry day. Jock waited for Margery at the church in Cockerton, but became increasingly worried as time passed without the bride. Outside the snow was so deep that the wedding car couldn't get through, and Margery had to walk almost a mile to the church in her wedding dress.

Jock arrived at No. 35 Squadron in November 1941, and his first operation, as 2nd wireless operator, took him to Essen. 'The next day the ground crew said to me, "Hey Jock" and they showed me a

piece of shrapnel. "That was right under your foot." I kept it in my pocket as a souvenir, but when I became a POW the Germans took it. You were always hit by shrapnel. That happened quite often.' Jock appreciated his new operational aircraft over his previous weapon of war. 'They moved a bit faster. When the Whitley was loaded up with bombs you thought it was going to fall out of the sky. There was a lot more space as well.'

Initially Jock flew with different pilots, but he soon became part of a more permanent crew, skippered by Canadian pilot Johnny Roe. Jock's operational tally rose, passing the twenty-trip mark and then towards the end of March 1942 he found his crew detailed for an attack on the German battleship *Tirpitz* lurking in a Norwegian fjord near Trondheim. For the attack the No. 35 Squadron Halifaxes were initially deployed north to operate from RAF Kinloss. On the way there, as they were flying near Aberdeen, Jock pointed out his house to Johnny Roe. Johnny swung the bomber around, took aim, flew down a hill straight at the house and pulled up just in time. A friend of Jock's, 'poor old Bill Shepherd', fell off his bike. 'We could have been up for court martial but och – it was fun.'

The raid of 30/31 March proved a failure. Cloud and mist hid the *Tirpitz*, which was not

Right Back (left to right) Jock Morrison, Johnny Roe, Jack Massie. Front (left to right), Jock's wife Margery, Cath Roe and Jock's sister Jean. *(John Morrison)*

Left Wreckage of Jock Morrison's No. 35 Halifax W1053 TL-G. *(John Morrison)*

found; six Halifaxes were lost, and forty-two Bomber Command airmen killed. Jock next found himself on an operation to find and sink the *Tirpitz* on the night of 27/28 April. This time the German warship was found and attacked, and Bomber Command lost a further five aircraft and thirty-three airmen, of which fifteen were killed. On 28 April analysis of reconnaissance photographs failed to find any damage to the *Tirpitz*, so crews were informed that a further assault would be carried out that night. The attack was planned in two waves: nine No. 76 Squadron Halifaxes and twelve Avro Lancasters from Nos 44 and 97 Squadrons dropping bombs from high level in the first wave and then fifteen Halifaxes of Nos 10 and 35 Squadrons, dropping mines from low level, in the second wave. The *Tirpitz* was found by the attacking aircraft, but again the raid proved unsuccessful, at a cost of two Halifaxes and crews. Johnny Roe, piloting Halifax W1053 TL-G, had been one of those No. 35 Squadron pilots who had lifted his aircraft from the

runway at RAF Kinloss that night and set course for Norway. The following day Halifax W1053 TL-G would be recorded as having 'failed to return'.

One Norwegian historian described it as the Second World War equivalent of the Charge of the Light Brigade, except on this occasion they used Halifaxes instead of horses. It was a suicide mission.

We had to fly at 150 feet above sea level into the fjord – the mouth about a mile wide and the cliffs one side at 800 feet and at the other side 400 feet. By the time you got to the top end of the fjord it was about 200 yards wide. How Johnny Roe ever got that plane out of there I do not know.

The Germans had filled the fjord with smoke and when we reached the point at which the *Tirpitz* was – it was supposed to be sheltering up against one of the sides – Reg Williams shouted that it had been swung round 90 degrees. Johnny responded, 'Right we'll go round again.' Just at that point we were hit and caught fire. Someone shouted to Johnny, 'Make for Sweden, it's only 40 miles away.' 'That's impossible,' Johnny responded. 'I've got very little control of the aircraft. Take your positions.'

We knew where we had to go. Dennis Butchart the engineer was in the second pilot position. Reg Williams, the navigator, myself and Rusty, the second wireless operator who was in the mid-upper turret, should have gone to the rest position. Reg and I did so but there was no sign of Rusty.

Before we crashed we opened the escape hatch and we always flew on operations with the steps to the hatch in place. I was still in communication with Johnny, I was plugged into the intercom and I could hear exactly what Johnny was saying and knew exactly when we were going to crash. When we did I was knocked out for a few seconds.

Jock had suffered a nasty cut to his upper lip and broken dentures. He started to climb the steps but was held back – he had forgotten to pull out the intercom.

Instead of just getting the helmet off, throwing it off, I went back down again. Reg went up the steps in front of me and just as he got out there was a fire flash – we were well and truly on fire then. His face and hands were badly burned. We dropped down to the side of the aircraft and a few seconds later Dennis came staggering out. It transpired he had a broken arm and broken ribs – we didn't know that then.

Dennis, clearly in considerable pain, managed to inform Reg and Jock that Rusty had been killed in the crash, crushed by the turret that had also injured and briefly trapped the distressed flight engineer.

Johnny Roe had managed to bring the burning Halifax down on to a frozen lake. 'Prior to the raid the pilots had seen a mock-up of the area, so they knew there were no flat areas where you could land but there were frozen lakes. Johnny tried to land on one of these but had no control over the speed.' The Halifax had skidded into a wood at the lake's edge, near two small farms, Elverum and Sørmo. The pilot had exited the wreckage on the starboard

side, and met with rear gunner Bill Parr. In the darkness they headed off east, with the intention of trying to make the Swedish border. Meanwhile, Jock and Reg, supporting Dennis, decided they needed help and set out through the snow towards some house lights.

From inside the nearby Sørmo farm Ingvald Arnstad had seen the flaming Halifax crash and, making his way to the wreckage to see what he could do, he came across Jock, Reg and Dennis. Ingvald beckoned for them to come to the house. They were met at the door by John Sørmo, taken inside and met by his wife, Anna. Dennis was laid out on a couch and, as Jock recalled 'they put a big cloth over my face and patched Reg up'. The airmen, who did not know any Norwegian, were keen to get away and make for Sweden, but requests for food and coats did not register with their non-English-speaking hosts. Meanwhile, the Sørmo's son Egil had been sent to find and bring back an English-speaking neighbour, Oddlaug Øvreness. When she reached the Sørmo farm, Jock and Reg asked for help to get away, as quickly as possible, and make for Sweden. They also requested a doctor be found for Dennis. Shortly after, with sandwiches and John Sørmo's and Ingvald's jackets, Jock and Reg set out into the snow. Ingvald accompanied the airmen for a while until he was

Left Johnny Roe
(right) and Bill Parr at
the Sandvika border
post shortly after
capture.
(John Morrison)

persuaded to return – he had already put himself in enough danger. Back in the farmhouse, the phone rang. It was the Germans asking questions, but the Sørmo family prevaricated. The patrol the Germans despatched mistakenly went to the wrong side of the lake. They asked a local whether the ice was safe to cross with their vehicle. He lied and said no. This bought Jock and Reg valuable extra time. As Jock and Reg set off into the mountains, a doctor came and tended Dennis, who was later taken to nearby Markabygd and handed over to the Germans.

Jock and Reg, 'with snow up to our knees', walked through the night and most of the day, 'until about 4 o'clock in the afternoon. We found this hut beside the lake and broke in. We slept there for about 24 hours. We left some money from our escape kit. It turned out we had left enough money to repair the lock ten times over.' As night was drawing in on 30 April the two airmen set out, once more, into the mountains heading east. 'When morning came we saw a farm, which we watched for about an hour to make sure no Germans were there.' Eventually they went and knocked on the door and were met by Mette and Odin Vikvang. 'The people were very kind and very frightened, but they gave us some sandwiches and helped us on our way.'

Returning to the mountains the airmen were still determined to reach Sweden, 'but Reg's hands, wrists and face were badly burned and it was getting obvious that he was in a bad way and in need of medical treatment'.

We foolishly, I suppose looking back, decided to come down off the mountains and go down on to the road. We trekked up the road and at about 9 o'clock at night, absolutely knackered, we decided we would have a rest and came off the road. Unfortunately we had left our footprints in the snow and just as we were settling down two work-men, on pushbikes, came along. They could see the footprints and when they looked up they saw us. They disappeared down the road and about 10 minutes later came with a German patrol, who saw us, aimed their rifles and said 'For you the war is over.' They did actually use those words.

Jock and Reg were taken by truck to a German border post near Sweden. Via Oslo, and transport to Berlin in a Junkers 52, Jock eventually arrived at DulagLuft for five days' solitary confinement.

It was the usual. One would come in and scream and shout and swear at you and the other would come in as nice as ninepence and offer you cigarettes and sweets. I told them name and number and that was it. No ill treatment. It was amazing the amount of information they could tell me about 35 Squadron that I didn't know.

A few days later Jock was moved to StalagLuft III at Sagan.

For the first 6 months you walked around in more or less a daze. You didn't look after yourself – well you looked after basics, but you weren't very interested in life. You were behind barbed wire and that was as far as you could get – no freedom. You were sleeping in a block about two and a half metres square. That was your space. Absolutely no privacy. You couldn't even change your mind without the person next to you knowing about it.

As the Allied aircrew POW numbers swelled with the continuation and escalation of the bombing offensive, Jock was part of a large body of NCOs moved from StalagLuft III east to StalagLuft VI at Heydekrug. In the spring of 1944, one particularly awful piece of news reached the 'kriegies' at StalagLuft VI concerning the break-out from StalagLuft III, immortalized as The Great Escape. Jock recalled the roll call that particular day.

That morning they shouted 'Raus, Raus, Raus – Roll call'. We went out and there were about twenty-four guards with machine guns on tripods, in the four corners of the parade ground. 'What the hell's going on here?' The German officer spoke to Dixie Deans, the Camp Leader. Dixie called us to attention and said, 'You will stay at attention as long as I tell you. I am going to read you something and you will stay at attention.' He read out the communication that he had received from the Germans – that from the group of officers that had escaped from StalagLuft III fifty had been shot while attempting to escape. The question was how many were injured. 'None.' We knew they had been murdered. Dixie said, 'You will stay at attention' and he held us at attention for about five minutes until we all settled down. If he hadn't, there would have been a massacre. We were so incensed we would have gone for the Germans, and they would have opened fire on us.

Owing to the advances of the Russian Army, the camp at Heydekrug was evacuated in July 1944. Jock initially went to StalagLuft 357 at Thorn and then, shortly after, with the threat of further Red Army advances, he was part of the evacuation west, across Germany, to Fallingbostel, where he came under the guard of the Wehrmacht. 'They were nasty at times.' Then in April 1945, with the Allies having crossed the River Rhine and advancing into Germany, a further evacuation. 'We were taken out and marched eastwards – billeted in barns and pig sties. All we had to eat was pig food. We were rather hungry by the time we crossed the River Elbe.' Two days after crossing the river the POWs were issued with Red Cross parcels, and Jock recalled 'marching up this leafy lane. We were sitting under the trees, diving into the food parcels and all of a sudden there was the sound of aircraft gun fire – cannon fire.' RAF Typhoons attacked and left 'about forty-six killed with four dying later – some RAF, some Army who had been POWs since May 1940. One of my friends was sitting with me. He dived one side of the tree. I dived the other side. He was killed. Such is life.'

After that, when we stopped we turned our overcoats inside out to show the white lining and made them into a large 'POW' in the fields. Unknown to us, after that attack, Dixie Deans got permission from the Germans to go through the British lines under a white flag and report to British officers what had happened. There were no more attacks on convoys, but Dixie, being the gentleman he was, kept his word. He could have stopped where he was with the British but he didn't – he came back to be a POW again.

Liberation finally came for Jock on 2 May 1945. 'We were released by some Wiltshires but told to stay where we were. Then after three days we were told to make our way to Luneberg.' They were ordered to find some German vehicles, but they needed to find someone who could drive. 'There were young men who could fly Halifaxes and Lancasters but they couldn't drive a car.' Eventually Jock with around thirty others found a wood-burning lorry and arrived at Luneberg. 'An Army sergeant said, "Who are you?" "We are prisoners of war." He said, "You're British aren't you?" We said "Yes". "Well you bloody fools you're ex-prisoners of war." I then knew we were free.'

Jock was flown back to England by Bomber Command as part of Operation Exodus, given new uniforms and sent home. Jock would be issued with his normal ration card and an extra one for malnutrition. 'When I went into the POW camp I was $10^{1}/_{2}$ stone. When I came out I was 7 stone. But I could not complain when I saw the lads that came back from Japan.'

When I got to Aberdeen it was about 10 o'clock at night on the Saturday. One of the lads, Jack, who was a POW with me in StalagLuft III, had been home for about a fortnight. He had gone out to see my mum, dad and Margery – who had moved up to Aberdeen in 1942. Jack was waiting for me, but Margery, who had been at Aberdeen station all day waiting, had gone home because it was so late and there would be no buses. I got off the train and there was a queue for taxis. I told them I had been a POW for three years. I got a taxi.

The arrival home proved highly emotional for Jock

– it still was when he recalled it sixty-five years later. 'When I got in, on the table was a plate of butteries. When we were on the POW march, there had been a number of Aberdeen lads and we said, "Och, we're starving." One said, "Hey would you like a buttery." And that's what I had when I got home.' ●

Left Trondheim (Stavne) Cemetery. Jock Morrison at the grave of 'Rusty' Russell, 2003. *(John Morrison)*

Below left Bomber Command veteran 'Jock' Morrison. *(Steve Darlow)*

CHAPTER THREE

FUTURES DENIED

LINZEE DRUCE

OPERATIONAL TRAINING UNITS (OTUS) WERE THE FINAL STAGE OF TRAINING FOR BOMBER COMMAND AIRMEN. AFTER COMPLETING TRAINING COURSES FOR THEIR SPECIFIC CREW POSITIONS, THE AIRMEN WERE POSTED TO OTUS, AND TRAINED TO FLY AS A WORKING CREW IN PREPARATION FOR JOINING AN OPERATIONAL SQUADRON. THE INSTRUCTORS AT THE OTUS WERE EXPERIENCED AIRMEN WHO HAD GENERALLY COMPLETED AT LEAST ONE, IF NOT MORE, TOURS FLYING ON OPERATIONS WITH A SQUADRON. A TOUR AT THE TIME OF THE EPISODE IN THIS CHAPTER WOULD GENERALLY BE THIRTY OPERATIONS. BEING POSTED TO INSTRUCT AT AN OTU WAS CONSIDERED BY THE RAF TO GIVE THE MEN A BREAK FROM THE STRESS AND STRAIN OF OPERATIONAL FLYING. IN SOME RESPECTS IT WAS JUST AS HAZARDOUS AS FLYING ON OPERATIONS OVER ENEMY-OCCUPIED TERRITORY, AND MANY LIVES WERE LOST IN TRAINING ACCIDENTS. THE CREW OF WELLINGTON R1646 PROVIDES ONE SUCH EXAMPLE OF YOUNG LIVES SACRIFICED AND VALUABLE EXPERIENCE LOST.

ONE TRAGIC TRAINING loss occurred on Monday, 19 January 1942, when a Vickers Wellington aircraft with a crew of eight young men failed to return from a flight from No. 20 OTU RAF Lossiemouth on the north-east coast of Scotland. Initially it was thought the aircraft had been lost at sea; however, that turned out not to be the case, although it would be some weeks later before the actual fate of the aircraft and crew was known.

The winter of 1942 was one of the worst that the north-east of Scotland had experienced, with heavy falls of snow and bitterly cold temperatures. In the middle of February, near the village of Braemar, some 60 miles south of Lossiemouth as the crow flies, Gamekeeper James Wright was out scanning the snow-covered landscape, checking for deer through his telescope. He noticed something unfamiliar near the top of a steep hillside in Glen Clunie. He couldn't be sure, but to him it looked to be the tail section of an aircraft.

On returning to the village of Braemar, James reported his sighting to the local policeman, Constable Gerrie, who in turn telephoned his HQ in Aberdeen to enquire if there were any aircraft reported missing in the Braemar area, to be told there were none.

James Wright, however, was convinced that he had seen something that warranted further investigation, and the following day a small search party of four set out from Braemar for Glen Clunie. Joining James and Constable Gerrie in the search were William Brown, a member of the local Home Guard, and his 15-year-old son, Andy Brown.

A lorry with a snow plough attached was used to drive as far along the road as possible, but the last 1 1/2 miles had to be covered on foot up a very steep hillside, with the men sinking at times waist deep into the snow.

The party finally reached the wreckage and could see that what James had spied through his telescope had indeed been the tail section of an aircraft, the glass of the rear gun turret glinting in the light. The

rest of the aircraft was buried under the snow, and it was obvious that it had been there for some weeks. There was no sign of life, and they were not able to identify the aircraft, as so little was above the snow. There was nothing the men could do but return to Braemar, where Constable Gerrie again telephoned his HQ and reported that the wreckage of an aircraft had been found.

The RAF sent a surveying unit from No. 56 Maintenance Unit out to the scene a few days later to investigate. The weather was extreme, making it incredibly difficult even to access the wreckage. Steps and paths had to be cut out of the ice and snow-covered hillside to reach the wreckage, which was identified as being that of Wellington R1646 from 20 OTU, missing since 19 January.

Left A young Andy Brown. *(Andy Brown)*

Below Jack Riley. *(Riley family archives)*

It took a further two months to complete the recovery of the crew, who were buried side by side in Dyce Old Churchyard near Aberdeen. They were named as:

Flying Officer James Williamson Thomson
DFC RNZAF, age 25, Pilot/Instructor

Sergeant Robert James Jackson RCAF, age 21, Pilot

Sergeant Michael Henry John Kilburn RAFVR, age 19, Pilot

Flight Sergeant Harry Joseph Kelley RCAF, age 23, Air Observer

Sergeant John Bernard Riley RAFVR, age 23, Wireless Op/Air Gunner/Instructor

Sergeant Beaumont Churchill Dickson RAAF, age 22, Wireless Op/Air Gunner

Sergeant Roy Alistair Milliken RAAF, age 22, Wireless Op/Air Gunner

Sergeant William Morphet Greenbank RAFVR, age 20, Air Gunner

Eight young lives wiped out in a training accident. Two of the young men had already completed tours flying on operations over enemy-occupied Europe. The young men onboard came from Australia, Canada, New Zealand, America and England. Before the outbreak of war these young men had been embarking on the start of their adult lives, completing their education and going on to work as accountants, bank clerks, scientists, salesmen. The war changed the direction they were to take with their lives and denied them the futures they deserved.

James 'Jim' Thomson was from Oamaru, Otago, in New Zealand. He was a member of the New Zealand Territorial Force for two years, studied accountancy at college and went on to work as a clerk with the Justice Department in Blenheim. In 1939 he applied to enrol with the RNZAF Civil Reserve of Pilots, who, in the event of war or a national emergency, are obliged to offer their services to the RNZAF.

In early 1940, Jim was mobilized with the RNZAF and began his training in New Zealand. He was commissioned as a Pilot Officer in August 1940 and in September he boarded a ship bound for the UK, where he arrived in November. After completing his pilot training in England, Jim was posted to No. 75 Squadron at Feltwell, arriving in March 1941.

During his time with No. 75 Squadron, Jim flew thirty-one operations over occupied Europe as well as searches over the Atlantic for German shipping. He was awarded the Distinguished Flying Cross for his courage during an incident in June 1941 on an operation to Düsseldorf, when the aircraft he was flying was attacked several times from the ground and air, resulting in it catching fire. The crew managed to extinguish the fire, and Jim was able to fly the aircraft back to base safely.

Right
Jim Thomson.
(Thomson family archives)

After completing his tour, Jim was posted to No. 20 OTU as an instructor. Jim must have been almost at the end of his posting when he died at the age of 25. His body was recovered from the crash site in April 1942.

The other instructor on board Wellington R1646 was John 'Jack' Riley, who came from Bentley, Yorkshire, in England. After leaving school, Jack had worked at Smiths Furniture Shop in Doncaster before volunteering for the RAF in April 1940.

In September 1940 Jack married Joyce Chapman at Askern village church in Yorkshire at a double wedding with Joyce's sister, Phyllis, who was also marrying an airman.

Jack trained as a wireless operator/air gunner and had completed the final stage of his training at No. 20 OTU at RAF Lossiemouth in April of 1941, unaware that he would be returning later that year as an instructor rather than under training. His first posting to an operational squadron was in May when he joined No. 218 Squadron at RAF Marham in Norfolk.

Keen to get his first operational trip over with, and having had four trips cancelled for various reasons, Jack finally set off on an operation to bomb Düsseldorf on the night of Monday, 2 June. On 4 June he wrote to his mother:

Naturally it was quite thrilling being our first trip – the ack-ack was pretty fierce and quite a few bursts were pretty near. However, it was very comforting to have our Wing Commander Squadron Leader Price as a pilot, as he has done about forty trips altogether – strangely enough I wasn't in the least scared during the trip, only thrilled and excited naturally.

Actually, this game is just a matter of luck; the majority of the blokes here have done over twenty trips. As you know, we have only thirty to do then we get grounded as instructors – I don't doubt for a second that I shan't come through this lot OK.'

Tragically Jack would lose his life just six months after writing this, while instructing at an Operational Training Unit.

Jack was to fly thirty-one operations with No. 218 Squadron, the majority with Squadron Leader

Left Jack Riley.
(Riley family archives)

Price as captain. Most of the operations were over Germany. Several operations were to the Channel port of Brest in France, and one to Turin in Italy. These operations were not without incident. On the night of 15 July, on an operation to Duisberg, the Wellington Jack was on board was hit by flak in the port wing, engine and several places along the fuselage. The rear turret was also rendered unserviceable by flak. No. 218 Squadron lost one Wellington on this operation, but Jack's landed safely back at base. The pilot, Squadron Leader Herbert Lawrence Price, was awarded the DFC for this operation.

In December 1941, after completing his tour of operations with No. 218 Squadron, Jack was posted to No. 20 OTU at Lossiemouth as an instructor, where he had trained earlier in the year. Jack was buried in March 1942. His family were not informed of his funeral until after the event had taken place, which caused them great distress.

Robert 'Bob' Jackson was one of two trainee pilots

The graves of
some of the crew
of Wellington
R1646 at Dyce Old
Churchyard.
(Linzee Druce)

Right Bob Jackson.
(Jackson family archives)

onboard Wellington R1646. Born in Birchcliffe, Scarborough, Toronto, in Canada, after leaving school Bob worked first as a clerk in a grocery store before joining the staff of the Royal Bank of Canada.

In December 1940, Bob enlisted with the Royal Canadian Air Force to train as a pilot and, after training first in Canada, he was posted overseas to Britain. In addition to leaving his parents and two sisters behind in Canada, he also left his sweetheart, Helen Garth. Bob and Helen had been seeing one another for three years but had decided not to become engaged because of the war.

Bob arrived in England in September 1941 and received instructions to proceed to No. 20 OTU at Lossiemouth in Scotland.

The telegram bearing the dreadful news confirming Bob's death and funeral arrangements was received by his mother, Ella, at her home in Birchcliffe, on 17 April, which was the date his funeral took place at Dyce Old Churchyard.

The other trainee pilot on board was Michael Kilburn, only child of Frank and Gladys Kilburn of Farnham, Surrey, in England. Michael was educated at Farnham Grammar School and was a member of the Cadet Corps. He was also a member of the Home Guard in Farnham.

After leaving school aged 18, Michael immediately joined the RAFVR to train as a pilot. He was completing his last two weeks of training at No. 20 OTU when he died.

Initially Michael was buried at Dyce Old Churchyard alongside the other seven members of the crew of Wellington R1646. His family in Farnham, however, wanted him closer to home.

On Saturday, 23 January 1943, one year and four days after his death, a funeral and reinterment took place at Green Lane Cemetery in Farnham.

Present at the funeral were his parents and immediate family, friends, colleagues, members of the Home Guard and the Farnham Grammar School Cadet Corps, as well as teachers from his former school. The coffin was draped with a Union Jack and, at the close of the committal, the Last Post and Reveille were sounded on a cornet played by a member of Farnham Home Guard.

The floral tribute laid by his family indicated the

Left Michael Kilburn. *(Via Linzee Druce)*

enormous loss they had suffered in sacrificing their only child and read 'in proud and undying memory of our only and beloved child Michael Henry John. Resting at last near us'.

Harry 'Joe' Kelley was born in Lakawanna, New York, USA, where his father worked in the steel industry. The Kelley family moved to Nova Scotia, Canada, when Joe was a small boy, and it was here that he grew up and was educated.

Joe attended Layola College and studied commerce and science at McGill University, Montreal. During the summer holidays Joe spent his time working at the Dominion Steel and Coal Corp. He was also a Cadet with the Canadian Officers Training Corps (COTC).

In October 1940 Joe joined the Royal Canadian Air Force to train as a navigator and, after undertaking most of his training in Canada, he was posted to Britain to complete the final stage at an OTU. Initially he was training at No. 11 OTU at RAF Bassingbourne, but on 6 January 1942 he was posted to No. 20 OTU at RAF Lossiemouth.

Linzee Druce at the
crash site of R1646
(Morten Moe)

Right Sergeant
Kelley. *(Kelley family
archives)*

Joe was buried at Dyce Old
Churchyard on 2 March 1942.
In May 1942 McGill University
awarded Joe a posthumous
Bachelor of Science degree,
which was received on his behalf
by his father, Harry Kelley.

William 'Bill' Greenbank was
born in Dent, Sedburgh, Yorkshire. Bill joined the Royal Air
Force Volunteer Reserve (RAFVR) and trained as
an air gunner. The final stage of his training was
at No. 20 OTU, where he sadly lost his life.

Initially Bill was buried on 2 March alongside
the other members from his crew at Dyce Old
Churchyard. His family later applied for permission
to have him buried in his local cemetery, and in
November 1942 his remains were reinterred in
St Mary's Cemetery, Windermere, Westmorland.

On 9 January 1942, ten days before he died, Bill
wrote a letter to his parents that he would leave
with his Commanding Officer for delivery only in
the event of his death. In it he wrote:

I have a feeling this will be my last letter
to you both. I have always admired your
amazing courage in the face of continual
setbacks. My death would not mean that
your struggle has been in vain. Far from
it, it means that your sacrifice is as great
as mine. I shall have lived and died an
English-man, nothing else matters one jot.

You must not grieve for me, I have
no fear of death, and I am prepared to
die with just one regret, and one only –
that I could not devote myself to making your
declining years more happy by being with you,
but you will live in peace and freedom and I shall
have directly contributed to that, so here again
my life will not have been in vain.

The letter was signed, 'Your loving son Bill', and a
PS was added to say, 'I was hoping this letter was
never to be sent.'

Two young Australians also perished on board
Wellington R1646 on 19 January. Beaumont
Dickson and Alistair Milliken were allocated
service numbers just two digits apart, indicating
they joined the RAAF on the same day at the same
time and place. They went on to attend the same
training courses together in Australia, sailed
together to Canada and were present at the same
courses in Canada before sailing to Britain just days
apart. Once in Britain they again frequented the
same training courses and arrived together at No.
20 OTU at RAF Lossiemouth in September 1941.

Beaumont Churchill Dickson was born in
Rockhampton, Queensland, Australia, and was
educated at Liechhardt Ward Boys School in
Rockhampton, where he was the Senior Swimming
Champion. On leaving school, he worked as a
junior clerk at Australian Estates in Rockhampton
and attended night school at the Technical College
to study typing, accounts and bookkeeping.

Beaumont joined the RAAF in October 1940
and undertook the early stages of his training in
Australia before being posted to continue training
in Canada.

For the next six months Beaumont passed
through training courses in Canada, learning the
skills required to be a wireless operator and air

Right Bill
Greenbank.
*(Greenbank family
archives)*

gunner. On completion he was posted overseas to Britain. After spending four weeks at Signals School at Yatesbury, he was posted to No. 20 OTU at RAF Lossiemouth.

Beaumont was buried on 2 March. Inscribed on his headstone were the following words: 'Enshrined in noble memory for evermore.'

Roy Alistair Milliken, known as Alistair by his family, was born in Mackay, Queensland, Australia. He began his education at school in Clermont, Queensland, before going on to the boys grammar school in Rockhampton and St Joseph's College, Nudgee, near Brisbane. After leaving school, Alistair studied accountancy at the Youth Employment Class at Rockhampton.

Like Beaumont Dickson, Alistair joined the RAAF in October 1940, and they trained together at the same units from this point onwards, sailing to Canada together, where they trained at No. 2 Wireless Training School, in Calgary and No. 2 Bombing and Gunnery School at Mossbank, Saskatchewan.

On 24 June 1941, Alistair married Mary Donahoe, a Canadian he had met during his stay in the country. Less than a month later he was on his way to Britain to continue his training, joining Beaumont Dickson at Signals School at Yatesbury, before they were both posted to No. 20 OTU at RAF Lossiemouth.

Alistair was buried on 2 March. Inscribed on his headstone were the words: 'He served his country well.'

The two young Australians who had joined the RAAF on the same day and who had trained side by side sadly both lost their lives on the same training flight in Scotland in January 1942.

The loss of the eight young men was felt deeply by their families. The mothers of all eight corresponded with one another for several years afterwards, sharing their grief, exchanging photographs of their sons, and offering one another comfort and support.

Another person who was profoundly affected by the loss of these young men was Andy Brown from Braemar. He was the 15-year-old boy who had accompanied the original search party that had located the crashed Wellington. Their loss played on his mind over the years, and he always felt that something should be done to remember them.

In 1999, Andy applied for permission to recover the engines of the Wellington from the hillside in Glen Clunie, with a view to using them to create a memorial to the crew. The engines were recovered with the assistance of the Argyll and Sutherland Highlanders, who, appropriately, had been the Regiment that guarded RAF Lossiemouth in 1942, and the RAF Sea King helicopter that is based at RAF Lossiemouth.

Finally, in August 2003, after years of planning and months of preparation, a memorial to the crew of Wellington R1646 was unveiled by HRH The Princess Royal, in the village of Braemar.

The memorial, one of the Pegasus engines from the Wellington standing on a granite plinth, is situated beside the Braemar War Memorial in the centre of the village, where it is visited by thousands of people every year. An information board with the history of the village nearby includes the story of Wellington R1646 and crew, so their memory will live on. ●

Far left Beaumont Dickson. *(Via Linzee Druce)*
Left Roy Alistair Milliken's wedding photo. *(Milliken family archives)*

Left Wellington R1646 Memorial in Braemar. *(Linzee Druce)*

CHAPTER FOUR

ON THE TOSS OF A COIN

JULIAN EVAN-HART

IT IS NOT DIFFICULT TO IMAGINE PEOPLE TOSSING A COIN TO SEE WHO DOES WHAT IN THESE MODERN TIMES. PERHAPS IT IS TO DETERMINE WHO DRIVES TO THE PUB TONIGHT OR WHICH TEAM GOES FIRST IN A COMPETITIVE SPORTS GAME. BUT JUST IMAGINE TWO INDIVIDUALS DOING THIS SIMPLE PROCEDURE TO ESTABLISH WHICH OF THEM WOULD BE CREDITED FOR HAVING JUST KILLED SIX MEN AND DESTROYED THOUSANDS OF POUNDS WORTH OF BRITISH GOVERNMENT PROPERTY.

IT WAS JUST a few days after the night of 21/22 December 1942 that two highly successful Luftwaffe nightfighter aces threw a coin up in the air to see what side it landed upon. On that occasion, seven decades ago, it was to determine which of them would get the credit for having destroyed an Avro Lancaster bomber. Of course, it being wartime, the destruction of such enemy personnel and their equipment was perfectly acceptable. The only problem was that Gruppen Kommandeur Hauptmann Wilhelm Herget and Leutnant Heinz Schnaufer had both claimed the destruction of a Lancaster bomber at the same time and remarkably in the same actual area. Both pilots had seemingly intercepted a Lancaster in the area of Geraardsbergen in what was the designated nightfighter region known as 'Raum 6'. However, the following morning it was quickly established that only one RAF heavy bomber had crashed in the district concerned. So it was decided the credit for the victory would be determined by the simple toss of a coin. Wilhelm Herget won and as a result was accredited with his sixteenth victory. As said, this act was simple, but behind it lay a myriad of connected emotions. It would be easy quickly to conjure up an image of heartless Germans tossing a coin to see who had not only destroyed an aeroplane but who had also destroyed and wrecked the lives of many people associated with its crew. But it is a good example to illustrate how detached the vast majority of aircrew, both Allied and Luftwaffe, were in all aspects of their job. Very few ever came into close contact with the remains of those they had killed. They might attend the crash scene next day to obtain a souvenir, but mostly at that stage all human remains had been cleared away. In essence this was a good thing. If they had started to get moral inroads into what they were doing, many surely would have had grave doubts and that would have slowly led to pondering ineffectiveness. This was total war, and neither side could afford to have such emotions erode away at their objectives. For the two Luftwaffe aces, the coin tossing was pretty much the end of the issue. But for many other people, the effects of what they had done would last in perpetuity. Although there was little choice but to decide who had done what, other than by using a coin, modern researchers are only too well aware that such a course can never be claimed to be accurate. So, some seventy years, later we are still left pondering who exactly it was who shot down this Lancaster on the night of 21/22 December 1942. For the purposes of this account, though, the author is of the opinion that it was indeed Heinz Schnaufer who destroyed this particular Lancaster.

One must consider that, approaching from different angles, it is just possible that both nightfighter crews had engaged and opened fire on the same Lancaster. One thing is for certain: despite the fact that Herget won the toss, a victory marking for this Lancaster was also still applied to the tail fins of Schnaufer's Messerschmitt Bf110. Perhaps Schnaufer never really accepted the outcome of the tumbling coin. Examining Schnaufer's report and

Below Sergeant Roden Pickford RNZAF (Air Gunner). *(Courtesy of the Pickford family via Cynrik De Decker)*

diagram of the incident, however, does seem to indicate someone who is very sure of his facts. One of the original Schnaufer tail fins, complete with its victory markings, can still be examined to this very day at the Imperial War Museum in London. There is also another Schnaufer tail fin from one of his Me110s, also showing victory markings, currently held at the Australian War Memorial in Canberra.

The following, therefore, is an account of the story of a No. 57 Squadron crew and their Lancaster Mk1 DX-P 'Peter', made possible by the work of the Belgium Aviation History Association (BAHA).

On the night of 21/22 December the RAF heavy bombers of Bomber Command were scheduled to attack Munich. This raid would involve a considerable effort, totalling 119 Lancasters, 9 Short Stirlings and 9 Vickers Wellingtons. Earlier in the evening the No. 57 Squadron Lancasters had departed from RAF Scampton and set course eastwards for their designated target. This battle-hardened squadron had been one of the very first to convert to the Lancaster bomber. Crossing the cold waters of the North Sea was always a dubious pleasure on the outbound journey and was little improved coming home, especially if your aircraft had suffered battle damage. But before then the RAF crews knew they also had to run the gauntlet

of concentrated flak and the ever prowling Luftwaffe nightfighters. The odds certainly seemed stacked against them. One of the 119 Lancasters out that night was a Mk1 version coded DX-P 'Peter' (W4234). On board DX-P were:

Flying Officer Ronald Alfred Bowles RAF, from Ealing, Middlesex, Pilot

Flying Officer Alexander Eric Mulholland RAF, Navigator

Sergeant Maurice Charles Pearman RAF, Bomb Aimer

Sergeant Arthur Leslie Abraham RAF, Wireless Operator

Sergeant John Arthur Drain RAF, from Bonnington in Kent, Mid-upper Gunner

Sergeant Cecil Raymond Stubbs RAAF, Flight Engineer

Sergeant Roden Pickford RNZAF, Rear Gunner

Right
A Lancaster taking off. This image was supplied by the Pickford family.
It is uncertain if it is Lancaster DX-P.
However, the author has included it on the grounds that in all probability it is.
(Courtesy of the Pickford family via Cynrik De Decker)

This was a very experienced No. 57 Squadron crew, and consultation with Sergeant John Arthur Drain's log-book reveals many interesting facts.

According to this document, Drain first flew with Pilot Officer Bowles on the night of 15 October 1942, when they had bombed Cologne. The next mission had been to Le Creusot to hit the Schneider works, but a bird smashed into the cockpit Perspex of Lancaster W4775 and wounded Bowles. No. 57 Squadron was also to be involved in several raids concerning Italian targets. These raids were very precarious, as the crews had to fly over the Alps and then decrease altitude heading for the Italian peninsular and on to the targets. On the raid to Genoa on 8 November 1942 W4775 and her crew, including Drain, had returned early because of engine problems. The same target was also chosen with moderately successful results on 13 November. Turin was also now a primary target, and Drain visited that city in W4775 on 20 and 28 November and again on 8 and 9 December 1942. His tenth and final mission would be undertaken in Lancaster Mki DX-P (4234) on the evening of 21 December 1942.

From Alfred, the brother of Cecil Stubbs, we learn that Sergeant Cecil Stubbs came from New South Wales and had previously been an auto mechanic who also loved to swim and surf. He sometimes worked as a volunteer with the coastguard. In June 1940 he submitted an application at the local recruiting office. He was accepted and, after training, he departed from Australia on 25 May 1940, finally arriving in Canada on 5 July. From here he eventually reached Britain on 30 August 1940 right in the thick of the Battle of Britain.

On the night of 21/22 December 1942, Lancaster DX-P thundered over the enemy coastline and headed towards the Reich. Flying in the cold dark skies the crew could on occasion make out other aircraft in the vicinity, and the ever-present threat of collision had to be seriously considered. The bomber stream droned on and on

– the noise clearly audible to those living far below in occupied Europe. At around 2230 hours the first signals appeared on the German Freya radar screens: the streams of incoming RAF heavy bombers had been detected and were being plotted. Five Messerschmitt Bf110 Luftwaffe nightfighters of 2./NJG1 consequently took off from the airfield of Sint-Truiden in northern Belgium and were later joined by several Bf110s from 1./NJG4 based at Laon-Athies in France. The nightfighters were directed to patrol an area that extended from Brabant to Oost-Vlaanderen, looking for potential targets as they flew further inland.

Ever waiting for the incoming RAF heavy bombers, these nightfighters included some very experienced crews from 1./NJG4 and 2./NJG1. Two of them consisted of Leutnant Heinz Schnaufer

and his Bordfunker Unteroffizier Friedrich 'Fritz' Rumpelhardt from Stab 2./NJG1 and Hauptmann Wilhelm Herget with his Bordfunker (most likely Oberfeldwebel Hans Liebherr) from 1./NJG4. Schnaufer and Rumpelhardt were flying that night in the Bf110 coded G9+CC. At around 2240 hours the darkened skies now contained numerous aircraft, and both sides were only too well aware that not all of these were friendly. Orbiting around were many Luftwaffe nightfighter crews, all intent on destroying their share of the RAF terror fliegers and their aircraft.

Unknown to the crew of DX-P, about a quarter of a mile in front of them coming in from port was

Right
Roden Pickford as
a POW (top row,
second from right)
*(Courtesy of the
Pickford family via
Cynrik De Decker)*

just such a Luftwaffe nightfighter – hidden deep in the gloom and unseen by the prying eyes of any RAF gunners. Of course this included Roden Pickford in the tail turret of DX-P, stuck far out behind his fellow comrades. At 2250 hours the nightfighter had actually just crossed right in front of their flight path. The German crew had spotted an aircraft heading towards them and swung round flying parallel trying to identify just what type of aircraft it was. As they carried on for some miles, it was not possible to make an exact identification, so the nightfighter followed at some distance. The gap between hunter and potential intended prey lessen-ed, as both were rocked about by the turbulence from other aircraft close by. The Luftwaffe crew could see their target.

Four very faint yellowish-white exhaust flames could be seen some distance out in front, occasionally blurred by streaks of passing cloud. This at least confirmed that the aircraft out in front was an RAF bomber. The crew in the Lancaster DX-P flew on, totally unaware of the extreme danger approaching from behind.

Suddenly the front of the Bf110 nightfighter flashed violently as its armament of two 20mm cannon and four MG17 machines spat out six streams of projectiles. These projectiles consisted of 7.92mm bullets and the larger 20mm cannon shells, all streaking away through the night air towards the Lancaster. The bomber's rear gunner and mid-upper gunner immediately spotted the glow reflected in the fleeting wispy cloud layer, as the streams of racer headed towards them. The night-fighter pilot also watched as the threads of glowing tracer terminated in a series of large brilliant white explosions and smaller flashes on the target. There was no time for the Lancaster's gunners even to respond before the ear-splitting explosions and rattling sounds echoed inside the giant bomber. In a split second the Lancaster's port inner and outer engines were disabled and the entire wing root area became a massive sheet of flame. Immediately, the giant bomber swung over to port and described an ovoid flight pattern, swinging round in a giant loop and crossing over its previous flight path. The crippled bomber then carried on with a direct flight path, still being shadowed by the nightfighter.

What happened to other crew members inside the bomber can only be guessed at, but unusually the only crew member to bail out was the tail gunner, Sergeant Roden Pickford. The survival of Roden Pickford perhaps indicates that the nightfighter did not attack from directly behind the Lancaster but from more of an angle off to the port side, the impacting shells and bullets possibly first striking the fuselage below the mid-upper turret, into the port wing root and progressing into the cockpit area. Apart from Pickford, all the other young RAF aircrew remained trapped, dead or dying in their bomber. Their huge crippled aircraft now assumed a heavy lean to starboard, before quickly entering a near vertical dive. As the stricken bomber plummeted earthwards, small sections of damaged airframe began to be stripped away. The whole flaming mass was roaring and shrieking as the wind tore through the damaged areas. As it fell further downwards, the flames around the mainframe assumed the shape of a giant descending teardrop, with a thin wavering 250-metre-long tail.

Far down below, several locals from the village of Sint-Maria-Lierde came outside to see what was happening and, looking upwards, saw the flaming mass coming down. Moments later the bomber containing six of its young aircrew and a full bomb

KILLED IN ACTION

SERGEANT CECIL RAYMOND STUBBS, previously reported missing, believed killed, is now reported killed in action on December 21. He joined the R.A.A.F. in June, 1940, and had 18 months service overseas. Before he enlisted he was a member of the Coastal Patrol, and was employed by McLeod, "Kelso and Lee." He was 28.

load smashed into the ground. Instantly, the huge propeller blades were crumpled, twisted and folded around the heavy engine blocks as they punched into the soft soil. Initially there was an ear-splitting explosion caused by the rupturing of the massive fuel tanks and then this was followed by a massive swirling and billowing fireball. DX-P had hit the ground with tremendous force, ramming wreckage to a depth of over 10 feet in the soil. However, the explosion that immediately followed unearthed this buried mass, ripping it upwards and spreading it far and wide over the locality, thus creating a massive crater in the process. As the fireball lessened, the crash site looked like a huge pyrotechnical display. It became topped with intensely bright glowing white arcs of flame as the numerous 4lb incendiary bombs began to detonate in the heat. Amid all this was the steady pop and spark-ridden crackle of exploding .303 ammunition. Both the Schnaufer and Herget crews radioed their respective airfields at the same time providing confirmation of a definite victory in the area 1 kilometre west of Steenhuize. Next morning, however, it was soon apparent that only one Lancaster had actually crashed in this area, coming down near the village of Sint-Maria-Lierde.

Immediately after the crash, several villagers began to investigate just what had happened out in the field. Certainly it was an air crash, but was it German or British? Approximately 400 metres away, Roden Pickford was discovered. He had collided with some high-tension cables, which damaged his parachute. Falling heavily, he had broken one of his legs. Eyewitnesses recalled that he was extremely tall and had fair hair. One of the villagers could speak a little English, and Pickford managed to inform him that he had bailed out of the plane that had just crashed. The following morning Pickford was taken into custody by some German soldiers. Some accounts state that he was taken back to the crash site in the morning to assist in identifying the remains of what was left of his colleagues. Pearman, Mulholland, Drain and Cecil Stubbs all rest in a communal grave. Bowles and Abraham, however, have individual grave plots in

Left Newspaper cutting announcing the death of Sergeant Cecil Raymond Stubbs RAAF (Flight Engineer). *(Cynrik De Decker)*

Left A grainy wartime photograph of the crash site of DX-P taken the following morning. The severity of the impact of Lancaster DX-P is all too obvious. *(Courtesy of the Pickford family via Cynrik De Decker)*

Aerial view of the
excavation of
Lancaster DX-P.
(BAHAAT)

the Geraardsbergen cemetery. A group of German soldiers was allocated the task of clearing the debris from the crash site.

....

Some fifty-seven years later just how effective they had been would become all too obvious. The war progressed and was finally over, and, as the decades rolled by, apart from their families the memories of these young airmen, as in so many cases, began to fade. As the years marched on, even the event of their huge Lancaster bomber crashing began to diminish in local memory.

Until the late 1990s this progression into the haze of historical records had carried on un-stopped. However, the crash site of DX-P was one of those scheduled to be investigated by BAHA. An early-stage investigation using metal detectors on the crash site had actually revealed two cigarette cases and a fire-black-ened coin that was found to be a British penny. So it was that one September morning in 1999 Dirk de Quick and his team arrived on the field where Lancaster DX-P had ended its days nearly six decades before. The site had been marked out and taped off as a security measure. The farmer Johan Vindevogel also arrived with his excavator at around 8 o'clock that morning. Everyone was tense, and it was, of course, unknown exactly what would be unearthed, unknown what still remained of a once-mighty RAF bomber. From the start of the dig all the excavated soil was sieved so that even the smallest parts from the huge aircraft could be recovered. By 0915 hours a signal flare pistol and a superb example of an oxygen bottle had already been re-covered from among much compressed airframe and smaller pieces. Then a large crushed container for the incendiary bombs was unearthed. Inside it were dozens of the counterweights for these small fire bombs. The dig was stopped to ensure that the

Right Small artefact recovered from the crash site of Lancaster DX-P. *(BAHAAT)*

ground was safe to continue and that no explosives or phosphorous traces were still present. When the dig was resumed later on, the excavation was widened, and more crushed bomb containers were located, along with a fire extinguisher that was discovered by Paul Callebaut. The extinguisher still bore a red painted label with yellow writing on it, even after having been buried for nearly six decades.

However, there was something rather unusual about the stratification of the items recovered. Even at the most severe of air crashes, the archaeology will have areas that make sense in relation to the shape and structure of the aircraft involved. In this case, however, the excavation was revealing a totally mixed and random series of artefacts. In addition, unusually, there were no larger sections such as the engines, and none of the guns was located. It was soon very obvious that the modern-day rescue archaeologists had been beaten to it by a unit of German soldiers some fifty-seven years before. They had meticulously dug out and recovered all the larger sections and the guns and had then backfilled the crater with the associated tattered jumble that lay scattered around.

To ensure that as good an archaeological excavation was undertaken, other exploratory diggings were also started, based on the findings of metal detector signals. These resulted in the recovery of some instrument faces, a cable cutter and numerous other fragments. Ironically it was a local gentleman called Marcel Vincke who came along to the site and brought with him one of the largest pieces to be seen that day. It was a lengthy part of spar that had been used as part of a door frame for the last thirty or so years. Another small excavation revealed the presence of some sizeable shattered sections of armour plating as well as numerous other pieces. Finally it was declared that all that was evident had been recovered, and all the artefacts were loaded up and taken away.

Now would begin the months of researching to find out where possible just what each part was. Of course, because of the corrosion of some artefacts, the dedicated conservation that would be required now had to begin before each artefact could be exhibited. However, the account does not end here. In May 2000 an impressive monument was inaugurated and dedicated to Lancaster DX-P and its crew. Part of the monument is formed from seven of the 4lb incendiary bomb counter-weights that were part of DX-P's original bomb load – the number seven was chosen so that one counter-weight would represent each crew member. At the inauguration ceremony, several relatives and members of the aircrew's direct families attended. Sadly, the sole survivor of this crash, Sergeant Roden Pickford, had passed away in 1987. However, his family most kindly and unexpectedly donated his medals, insignia and flying cap to the BAHA collection. In return, BAHA was honoured by being able to give all relatives who attended a piece of Lancaster DX-P.

Every year on the evening of 21 December BAHA members gather around the monument, and, at the exact time that the Lancaster crashed into the adjacent field, a large torch is turned on.

This solitary beam of light that now probes into the dark skies is yet another beacon of commemoration that BAHA and so many other aviation archaeologists strive to achieve – a solitary beam of light that, along with all the conserved artefacts, helps to shine as a timeline all the way back to that other dark December night some seven decades earlier.

In May 1945 Heinz Schnaufer was captured by the British at Eggebek in Schleswig-Holstein. He was released later in the year and returned to Calw, eventually taking over the family wine business. However, Schnaufer's real passion, as always, was flying, so he shortly departed for South America. In order to do this he crossed into Switzerland to arrange travel with the relevant consulates, but he entered Switzerland illegally and was arrested. After spending six months in internment, he was released and once again returned to the family business. The business was soon flourishing. However, on 13 May 1950, during a wine-purchasing trip to Bordeaux, he was involved in a collision with a lorry. The lorry driver failed to observe the correct right of way and, in the ensuing collision, heavy gas cylinders on the back of the lorry broke free and crashed down on Schnaufer's car. One of these cylinders struck Schnaufer on the head, and he was taken to hospital.

Two days later the top-scoring Luftwaffe night-fighter ace, who had 121 victories (114 of them four-engine bombers) and who had become known as the 'Spook of St Trond', was dead.

The No. 57 Squadron motto is 'CORPUS NON ANIMUM MUTO', which translates as 'I change my body but not my spirit'. It is unusual for a dedicated motto to be as appropriate as it is to these six young men who were killed on board Lancaster DX-P so long ago. Their bodies may indeed have changed but their spirit certainly lives on and indeed will never change, assisted in no small way by the dedicated efforts of the Belgium Aviation History Association and its members. ●

Left
Heinz Schnaufer.
(Courtesy of the Schnaufer family)

Left Relatives of some of the DX-P aircrew stand adjacent to the memorial upon its inauguration.
(Courtesy of the Pickford family via Cynrik De Decker)

CHAPTER FIVE

A DISASTROUS NIGHT

STEVE BOND

THE MAIN FORCE ATTACK ON LEIPZIG ON THE NIGHT OF 19/20 FEBRUARY 1944 TURNED OUT TO BE A DISASTER FOR BOMBER COMMAND AND IN TERMS OF LOSSES IT WAS SECOND ONLY TO THE NOTORIOUS NUREMBERG RAID JUST OVER FIVE WEEKS LATER. A FORCE OF 294 LUFTWAFFE NIGHTFIGHTERS ATTACKED THE BOMBER STREAM FOR THE LOSS OF 17 OF THEIR OWN NUMBER AND 78 BOMBERS, 44 AVRO LANCASTERS AND 34 HANDLEY PAGE HALIFAXES – 9.5 PER CENT OF THE ATTACKING FORCE. AMONG THE LATTER WERE TWO HALIFAX IIS OF NO. 102 SQUADRON. SERGEANT LES GIDDINGS WAS THE FLIGHT ENGINEER ABOARD ONE OF THEM, BECOMING A PRISONER OF WAR ALONG WITH EIGHT MORE FROM THE TWO AIRCRAFT, THE OTHER FIVE CREW MEMBERS LOSING THEIR LIVES. FOLLOWING THIS RAID, BOMBER COMMAND PERMANENTLY WITHDREW THE MERLIN-POWERED HALIFAX II AND V FROM OPERATIONS OVER GERMANY, AS NO FEWER THAN SIXTEEN OF THESE VARIANTS WERE AMONG THE LOSSES.

LIKE SO MANY other young men, Les Giddings felt the need to do his bit, and in 1942 he volunteered for aircrew duties, being enlisted on 17 August. He found himself streamed for flight engineer training at St Athan in south Wales, passing out in early 1943. 'Well let's say they gave me a brevet with an E in it, three stripes, and I'd never been off the ground in my life.' Unlike the rest of a heavy bomber crew, flight engineers were not sent to Operational Training Units to crew up, and Les's next move was to the Halifax-equipped No. 1652 Heavy Conversion Unit at RAF Marston Moor in Yorkshire, which at that time was under the command of Group Captain Leonard Cheshire, who was being rested from operations. Les actually flew a cross-country flight skippered by Cheshire, and in September, with a total of just twenty-six flying hours under his belt, he was posted with the rest his crew to No. 102 (Ceylon) Squadron at RAF Pocklington, again in Yorkshire.

Their first operation was to Kassel, and they subsequently visited Berlin twice, and had completed seven of their required thirty ops by the time of the Leipzig raid. So, just before midnight on 19 February 1944, Halifax II JN972 DN-Y got airborne. The full crew on that fateful night was:

Flight Sergeant Kenneth Cummings RCAF, from Ottawa, Pilot

Sergeant Leslie G. K. Giddings, Flight Engineer

Pilot Officer O. P. J. McInerney RCAF, Navigator

Flight Sergeant George Charles Clark from Kenton, Middlesex, Air Bomber

Sergeant Norman Frank Lingley from Teddington, Middlesex, Wireless Operator

Sergeant Robert Patrick Rees Mid-upper Gunner

Sergeant John Torrance from Bonnybridge, Stirlingshire, Rear Gunner

'We thought it was going to be easy, because we were making a direct approach to Berlin, and ahead of us were Mosquitoes. Then we were starting an attack on Berlin, and when we got near Berlin we turned starboard, we were going to attack Leipzig. But it all went wrong.'

A diversionary operation by Short Stirlings to lay mines at Kiel was only partially successful in drawing off Luftwaffe nightfighters and, as the Main Force crossed the Dutch coast, there were still many fighters in the area awaiting them. Those that had been sent to Kiel were able to rejoin the main defensive force quite quickly, with the result that the Main Force was under almost constant attack all the way to the target area. In addition, winds had been much stronger than forecast, and many of the bombers arrived too early and were forced to orbit and await the arrival of the Pathfinders, not least because the target was cloud-covered. Many more aircraft were lost to flak and four were lost to mid-air collisions during this time.

By 0240 hours Ken Cummings had reached the area of Sülingen, south of Bremen, and was still a long way from Leipzig when the Halifax was hit by cannon fire from a Messerschmitt Bf110G flown by Oblt Heinz Ferger of 3./NJG 3. He thereby claimed

Left Flight Sergeant Ken Cummings. *(Via Les Giddings)*

Left Halifax II JD206 DY-T No. 102 Squadron, RAF Pocklington, 22 June 1943. *(Air Historical Branch)*

his first of four victories that night, all within the space of just over half an hour. (He would go on to achieve twenty-seven victories by the time he was killed in action on 10 April 1945, when he was shot down by a Mosquito while landing at Lübeck.) Les vividly remembered the attack: 'It took out the port outer engine, then the port inner, and set the tanks on fire. Thankfully they still had fuel in them, because the shots came up from underneath, if they'd been empty they would have exploded.' Mortally wounded, the Halifax was doomed; it was an emergency bail-out.

I couldn't get the skipper's parachute clipped on him, because he had the stick pulled back so hard. He let go and I tried to clip it on; as a result the aircraft became uncontrollable. He ordered me to bail out, and he knew he wasn't going to be able to get out. The mid-upper gunner was married to a WAAF; he was about 19 I think. She got hold of me one night and she said, 'You help him out if anything goes wrong', and I said I would. But as I ran past his turret, he was out of it, and I said, 'For Christ's sake come on Taffy', because the whole port wing was a sheet of flame, and I didn't see him again. As I opened up the door, the rear gunner was out of his turret and plugged in at the door, on the intercom; I pulled his hat back and said 'For God's sake you can see the flames!' They were past his turret by that time, and whether he got out or not, I don't know, so I went out of the entrance door.

Of the seven crew, only Les and McInerney, the navigator, were able to get out. The remainder were all killed when the aircraft hit the ground on Siedeneer Moor, south-east of Sülingen. Their bodies were subsequently recovered by the Germans and laid to rest in Sülingen, before being moved later to Hanover War Cemetery.

Les found himself drifting down under his parachute.

I don't know whether I had become unconscious, because we must have been at about 21,000 feet when we bailed out. But I thought I ought to have been able to see the plane; I looked all round but I couldn't see it. So I thought 'what to do?' The first thing I noticed was how quiet it was without the roar of the engines. The pilot, the flight engineer, and wireless operator, we all got heat, the rest didn't get much, so we didn't need to wear flying suits and stuff like that, so I could get my hand inside my top pocket, got my fags out and had a cigarette – it must have been minus 25 to 30 degrees. The thing was, when the cigarette got down to the stub, I thought if I throw it away it'll go up and set fire to the parachute, so I managed to drag one foot up and stub it out on it!

Les came down near a village, and there were a few Luftwaffe people passing through who took charge of him, having watched him come down and waited for him to land. The only available place they could take him to was the local inn, so they sat in the bar and Les went to sleep with his arms tied.

I woke up and looked around, and there was this 'Your country needs you' SS poster; I thought 'Oh Christ Almighty!' A policeman turned up with a pony and trap, and took me to the railway station. When I got there, my navigator had been carried piggy-back by a prisoner of war, and we were the only two survivors.

They were taken to a Luftwaffe airfield at Diepholz (from where Les was subsequently flown back to England following liberation). The navigator had broken his leg and left arm when he landed and was taken to hospital. Les was put in a cell and in the one next to him was a Flight Sergeant Pearson, the navigator of a No. 207 Squadron Lancaster that had also fallen victim to a nightfighter attack. The following evening Les was taken to the guard-room. 'There were their equivalent of our WAAFs, coming in and booking out and pointing me out, "Englischer flieger". There was quite a little "Look, they're sending boys" sort of thing, because I only looked about 15 or 16.'

On the following day an air-raid siren sounded around lunchtime, and many Messerschmitts roared off into the air as the US 8th Air Force attacked the airfield. The German guards ran off to take cover and left the prisoners in their cells.

The bombs were getting bloody close and all the

tiles were blown off the walls; the building was on fire. The guardroom I'd been sitting in that night had also been hit. It blew the door out and I managed to prise it open and get outside. They grabbed hold of me, made me be a stretcher-bearer along with three Germans for a Luftwaffe bloke using one of the doors from the guardroom; he had a hole in his back you could put a fist in. Then we heard the whistle of more bombs coming down; the three Germans left him and we jumped into a ditch. Somebody jumped in by the side of me; it was this bloke with a big hole in the back! The three Germans with me who had been

because we'd been told that if you were there for more than seven days you must be giving them information, and I actually had nobody to talk to, apart from the feller with the Red Cross letter, which I refused to sign. They said 'Well, your parents will never know. This is the only way you can get through, through the Red Cross, and we don't open it.' What I didn't like about the interrogation was the fact that the Luftwaffe bloke who was interrogating me knew more about my squadron than I did. He could name names, and all things like that, and showed me the list of what was shot down.

Halifax II DT743 DY-O No. 102 Squadron, RAF Pocklington, 19 June 1943. *(Air Historical Branch)*

carrying him decided they'd had enough, and pushed me underneath the barbed wire and off we went; we left the poor bloke there. The next bombs that came down showered us with dirt, and he must have been hit on top of the head, poor devil. Then I was taken back to the cells and consequently it was a long time before the nav and myself got to interrogation.

In the end I had to ask for interrogation,

After interrogation, they were released into the main compound, and Les had become POW No. 2196. 'We actually looked like holiday-makers, because we were issued with a cardboard suitcase from America, with everything in there; shirts, cigarettes, chocolate, everything.' They were walked down to the railway station and put in carriages divided into three parts, that had painted on the side '40 men or 8 horses'.

Right: 18 February 1944. A Handley Page Halifax in flames after crash-landing on its return to base after a raid on Germany. A truly disastrous night for Bomber Command.
(Air Historical Branch)

Thirty-odd of us – I was the only RAF chap, the rest were Yanks – were in one-third and the German guards were in the other two-thirds. The guards were First World War men, I should imagine, because they looked it, and they suddenly called me over and said 'Tommy?' because I had a different colour uniform. 'You Tommy?' and I said 'Yes.' 'Tipperary', and they finally got it across to me, they wanted me to sing 'Tipperary'. So I sang it, and from then on, because they had some bread, I ate; they wouldn't give anything to the Yanks.

The train journey lasted for about nine days, finally arriving at StalagLuft VI at Heydekrug, where camp leader for the British was Flight Sergeant Dixie Deans, who had been a POW since 1940, spoke perfect German and was frequently able to get prisoners out of bad situations. 'Heydekrug was still being used as a prison camp after the war. When I was flying in the airline, we used it to help us navigate coming out of Swedish air space en route to Russia; 35 years after the war had ended.'

Bloody cold it was. They called a special parade one day, and they lined us up three sides of the square, which was unusual. They brought in machine guns and they placed them facing each of the three sides, and then we thought 'What the hell's going on?' There was snow on the ground, and the Commandant announced that there'd been a big escape from Luft III at Sagan (the camp to which McInerney had been sent) and fifty had been killed. We started shouting out 'How many wounded?' 'No wounded.' So we knew they'd been executed. Well we snowballed the bloody machine guns, and they didn't want to shoot us, the Luftwaffe, so they evacuated, and Dixie was calming us down.

In July the Germans sent 3,000 British NCOs to Camp 357 at Thorn (Toruń) in Poland, where they were mixed with army prisoners. 'What surprised us was in Heydekrug we had been locked in every night, shutters put across the windows and lights out. But in this camp, as long as we kept to the footpaths, we could go out and go to the toilet and come back into the billet.' As the war moved towards its closing stages, the POWs could hear the Russian guns, and they began to hope they could soon be liberated, but in mid-August they were moved to Stalag XI-B at Fallingbostel.

The Germans tried to march us up into Denmark.

Part the way up there they realized that we were clogging the roads up; they turned round and started marching us back. Then I think it was rocket-firing Typhoons of the RAF that came in and killed any people walking towards the front. They shot our column up, killed I think it was thirty-odd prisoners and eight guards; but the pilots didn't know we were prisoners. Then they took us back to Diepholz, I had a look at my old cell – and then to Fallingbostel.

Just down the road from us was a working camp for other ranks; they wouldn't allow us out to work. We could go out some of us, because it was a very cold winter, and the sick bay had no heating, and Dixie said 'Yes, we could sign a parole, and we could go and get wood.' So I did that rather than hang around the camp all day. When the Red Cross parcels ran out, we really knew it. The Luftwaffe men were not bad to us; not good, but not bad, because they were frightened of the SS who, without telling them, would suddenly put on a search of the camp. But, they would first of all move into the German quarters and kick them all outside, kick them out of the guard boxes, and check to see if they'd been trading with us; then they would check us.

We had some very smart cookies in the camp. Once, the SS checked us against our photographs and ID; then we were sent back to the barracks and locked in. At the end of the day – don't ask me how it was done, I've no idea – 200 of the identity cards had disappeared, and the Germans never did know, to the end of the war, how many people were in that camp. I never met up with the navigator again, he went to an Oflag. He was Canadian, much older than the rest of us; he was an old man, he was 33. My skipper was 21, I think on 17 February; he was dead on the 20th.

We were finally liberated by the British, but we still had to hang about in the camp while arrangements were made to get us home. The troops were ordered to keep us in, but they were British troops, they were not going to shoot us, so we just walked out. We got into Fallingbostel and found a wood-fired fire engine, which we nicked, fired it up and drove around the countryside looting; what we really wanted was eggs. Fallingbostel was about 11 kilometres from the concentration camp at Bergen-Belsen; I never want to see a sight like that again. They kept us well outside the barbed wire, but the stench was appalling, and the bodies were lying around, must have been thousands of them (the soldiers put on their guard's capes and gas masks). I was surprised that the SS were still there, but a lot of them didn't survive. The troops used bulldozers to push the bodies into the graves, and a lot of these SS people got hit on the back of the head with a rifle butt and covered over, you know.

Finally returning to England, Les stayed on in the air force for a while before being demobbed. A few years later he decided he did not take to civvy street and tried to re-enlist.

They said they were full of flight engineers, so I went down to Bath to join the army, and a few weeks after I joined I got a letter from the RAF saying 'Come back.' Too late, I'm in the army; I ended up as a glider pilot flying Horsas at Abingdon. Then I got back into the air force as a flight engineer again and served on Sunderlands, Lancs and Hastings.

After a total of twenty-three years' service, Les started a second career with Britannia Airways and Monarch Airlines, retiring in 1981 to live in Wing, Buckinghamshire, after 17,000 flying hours. He then became a staunch supporter of his local branch of the Aircrew Association and died in March 2008. ●

Left Bomber Command veteran Les Giddings. (*Steve Bond*)

CHAPTER SIX

STIRLING RESISTANCE OP

AMONG THE MANY TYPES OF OPERATION FLOWN BY BOMBER COMMAND, SOME OF THE MOST HAZARDOUS INVOLVED LONE AIRCRAFT FLYING SUPPLIES TO SUPPORT RESISTANCE FORCES IN OCCUPIED EUROPE, FLYING AT A MUCH LOWER LEVEL THAN WAS USUAL FOR BOMBING AND THUS BEING HIGHLY VULNERABLE TO GROUND FIRE. ONE SUCH OPERATION INVOLVED SHORT STIRLING III EF147 WP-J OF NO. 90 SQUADRON FLYING FROM RAF TUDDENHAM, WHICH WAS SHOT DOWN BY LIGHT FLAK ON A SPECIAL OPERATIONS EXECUTIVE (SOE) OPERATION ON THE NIGHT OF 5/6 MARCH 1944. ALL THE CREW SURVIVED THE SUBSEQUENT CRASH-LANDING IN NORTHERN FRANCE AND ALL BUT THE REAR GUNNER, WHO WAS CAPTURED, SUCCESSFULLY EVADED CAPTURE UNTIL ALLIED GROUND FORCES LIBERATED THEM SIX MONTHS LATER. SERGEANT RICHARD WENSLEY WAS THE STIRLING'S FLIGHT ENGINEER.

Born in 1924, Liverpudlian Richard Wensley volunteered for RAF service when he was 18 years old.

When you are that age, I don't know why but everybody wanted to go in the Air Force. I hate water so I didn't want to join the Navy and I saw the First World War scenes from the trenches and I thought 'God, I don't want that, going through mud.' The Air Force appealed, but you don't realise when you are a lad. Until you are actually over a target, the flak is coming up and the aircraft is going from side to side, then you think 'Bloody hell, I must be bloody stupid.'

Richard left school at the age of 14 and spent some time in the Air Training Corps; he wanted to be a wireless operator and did all his wireless training in

Wratting Common in Cambridgeshire, where he was crewed up. When he reported to the Sergeants' Mess with other new arrivals, they were told: 'OK boys, now unfortunately there is no bed for you at the moment. But there will be plenty for you tomorrow.' There were indeed plenty of beds, because the Squadron was losing a lot of aircraft at that time. Over the first three nights after Richard arrived at Wratting Common they lost five aircraft and thirty-five men; as he said:

Life was so bloody cheap. They used to say to us that all the training that we had done had got us this far, so we were not to even think about opting out otherwise our cards would be marked and we would be known for a lack of moral fibre. There were some blokes who got infected, it wasn't very nice but you just had to get on with it.

Below Stirling III EH906 XY-T C Flt No. 90 Squadron, RAF Wratting Common. *(Steve Bond)*

the ATC. However, when he enlisted, the interviewer said, 'Oh that's a shame really because we have too many wireless operators. But we are short of flight engineers.' Richard said that he didn't think he was clever enough, but he was given a test to see if he was suitable. He remembered being asked 'Who was the Viceroy of India?' He then began training with Rolls-Royce in Derby, moving on to St Athan in south Wales for six months.

At the end of the course in late June 1943 he was posted straight to No. 90 Squadron at RAF

Richard was first crewed with a pilot who the rest referred to as 'the turn-back king'.

There were four or five operations that we were going on and he had a heart attack, he had this, he had that and we were turning back all the time because he didn't want to go. I wasn't very unhappy about that to be honest, but eventually we got fed up with him and the WAAFs said 'Hello, what are you returning for this time?' So the crew went to see the CO to say we didn't

Right
Richard Wensley.
(Richard Wensley)

want to fly with him. They gave us a new pilot, who was the exact opposite unfortunately; Joe Edinborough was best described as 'shit or bust'.

All crews found their aircraft to be cold, draughty and uncomfortable; the Stirling was no different in that respect. The Squadron was on ordinary Main Force bombing, and Richard's first trip was to Nuremburg, followed by the long haul to Turin, but his later operations were mainly gardening (mine-laying). 'On one particular long distance operation we flew past Sweden, going up to the Baltic; we saw a line of interned Flying Fortresses in Sweden.' It was decided that, because the Stirling could not fly high, with the Lancasters and Halifaxes above them, they would be switched to special duties. This primarily involved flying to many different locations in France and dropping arms and ammunition for the Maquis both to support their usual harassment of the enemy and to start building up for the Normandy invasion. During briefing for the operation on the night of 5/6 March 1944, the wing commander told the crews that 'the target is likely to be overcast with cloud when you get there' (they relied on seeing flashlights in the fields to identify the drop zone); 'if you can't see where you are going, and you can't see the flashlights, then just get up to height and come home, because your aircraft is more valuable than messing about'. The operation involved a total of forty-nine Stirlings and seventeen Halifaxes on special duties operations.

At 2130 hours Stirling III EF147 WP-J took off from RAF Tuddenham in Suffolk, to where the Squadron had moved in October 1943. The crew were on their fourteenth operation, and comprised:

Warrant Officer Joe Edinborough,
Pilot

Flight Sergeant Norman Cartwright,
Navigator

Flight Sergeant P. A. Tansley,
Air Bomber

Flight Sergeant C. J. Singer,
Wireless Operator

Sergeant Richard Wensley
Flight Engineer

Flight Sergeant C. W. Walmsley RCAF,
Mid-Upper Gunner

Flight Sergeant L. E. Cox RCAF,
Rear Gunner

It was especially cold going over the coast on this particular operation, and they descended on course to fly to where they should have seen the flashlights, but they saw nothing, even though they were down to about 3,000 feet. The orders then were to just turn round and go back home, and they started to gain height, but the pilot told the crew that he would go back to the coast and get a dead reckoning of where they should be. As they got nearer to the coast at low level, the aircraft was hit by flak, and suddenly it was on fire. The pilot did not realize this at first, as he sat at the front with a curtain between him and the crew. Obviously those down the back could see it, so when Joe Edinborough said, 'Right let's get up to height,' Richard told him to 'open your bloody curtain Captain', which he did, and, seeing the intensity of the fire, said: 'Jesus, get into ditching positions.' That meant the crew got up against the spar, with their backs against it, and prepared to crash, since they were not high enough to bail out by parachute. Luckily the area that they came down in, east of Abbeville in the Pas-de-Calais in France, was clear of any villages and towns and was open country-side, but with no trees to impede the progress of the stricken Stirling as Joe put it down virtually blind on its belly.

All seven of the crew escaped without injury from the aircraft, which by now was almost completely engulfed in flames. Singer, Walmsley and Cox buried all the Mae Wests and harnesses in a nearby wood, and they now had to decide what to do. The standard instructions were to split up and travel in seven different directions, find their own way to a farm, give themselves up to the local farmer, and say that they were English aviators.

Of course being the cowards that we were, we ended up in the woods and went to sleep because we were terrified. This was near the village of L'Étoile, and we saw lights in several houses but decided to stay in the woods. We stayed there all the next day and some of the villagers brought us food and coffee in the evening.

The crew then headed east but had to go more towards the north-east because of German searchlights. In the early morning they found a farm in the area of Bernaville and hid in the hay loft. They asked the farmer for help, but he was very frightened and, although he gave them all some food, he told them they could not stay there for longer than one day.

They then decided they had to split up into three pairs, with one on his own. Richard paired up with Norman Cartwright, the navigator from the Lake District. The captain and the bomb aimer headed

west together, as did the wireless operator and the mid-upper gunner, while Flight Sergeant Cox, the rear gunner, said he wished to go on his own (he was to become the only member of the crew to be captured). They all then headed off south, hoping to pick up the River Somme, finally separating at Berneuil. Richard and Norman found another barn and fell asleep in it, where they were discovered by a labourer who they asked for help. He took them to a farm near the village of Vignacourt, where they stayed for just over two weeks, during which time they were joined by two other RAF evaders.

By late May the rest of the crew had been able to make their way back to England with the help of the French underground, but Richard and Norman were still in hiding. However, with the help of a sympathetic gendarme and a local doctor, they did contact the Resistance, which arranged to move them to Flixecourt, where they initially lived over a shop with three other airmen. They were put in the care of farmer Albert de Courtois. He might well

Right Richard Wensley's forged identity card as Emile Dufour. (*Richard Wensley*)

Left Flixecourt's hidden airmen including Richard and Norman after liberation. Flight Lieutenant Jeka holding the flowers. (*Richard Wensley*)

have turned them in, because they found out much later that he was taking bribes from the Germans and collaborating with them, so perhaps he decided to look after the airmen as his sort of safeguard. After the liberation, when he might well have been shot for being a collaborator, he was able

to say: 'Well I've looked after these airmen.' Richard, Norman and the other Allied airmen worked on the farm from 26 May to 2 September 1944, and Albert organized forged identity papers for Richard in the name of Emile Dufour.

I can remember the soup that we had at the farm, it was the best soup I have ever tasted; it was a

vegetable soup and that is the main thing that I can remember about the little French woman who made it. They also organized a secret party for my twentieth birthday on 15 June; everyone in the town was involved in keeping us hidden.

There were about seven or eight blokes hiding in the village. Five of us were in a secret room at the top of the co-op shop in the village; it was marvellous. One family that we stayed with was Madame Miannay and her son and daughter. She had asked me if I could find out what had happened to her husband Guy; sometimes they weren't told if they were killed or missing in action, so she just didn't know. His name is on the memorial in the village as he never did come back.

The others hiding with them were Flight Lieutenant Jeka, a Polish fighter pilot, and Flying Officer James and Sergeant Robertson, both Halifax crewmen from No. 35 Squadron, Path Finder Force, at RAF Graveley. James and Robertson were captured by the Gestapo on 27 August and taken to Abbeville, being badly beaten by their guards.

Although the area was remarkably free from large numbers of German troops, there were still some dangerous times.

The biggest scary moment was when an aircraft crashed outside the village and I thought there's

Left
Madame Miannay who hid Richard and Norman for a time, with her son. (*Richard Wensley*)

Right
Richard Wensley and
Norman Cartwright
during their time as
farm labourers in
Flixecourt.
(*Richard Wensley*)

Right Richard
Wensley, right, with an
unknown airman in
the yard of Flixecourt
Co-op.
(*Richard Wensley*)

going to be a search now for the crew of that aircraft. But Albert said, 'Oh don't worry boys, I'll hide you.' He put the two of us in a barn, under the hay, and we were there for a few hours. I started to get a bit edgy and I said to Norman, 'I'm sorry Norman, I can't stand this, I've got to make a run for it.'

They decided to make a break, whatever happened. They were no longer in uniform at this stage, but wore labourers' clothes, since they were working on the farm (including, at one point, planting potatoes alongside a V1 launch site). As they left the farm heading out towards the countryside, a young German sentry stopped them and said 'Monsieurs, passes...'. Richard responded with all he could think of to say: 'Pas de compris, pas de compris'; how we got away with it I don't know. A scruffy pair of bloody labourers, we just walked away and he let us go; you would think he would shoot you in the back. They were just ordinary blokes, they weren't like a storm-trooper or a Nazi, just an ordinary guy; we just walked away, so that was that.'

They returned to the village in the evening and went back to working on the farm. It took the Allied armies a further three months to get from where they landed on the beaches up to where the crew were hiding in the Pas-de-Calais. On Liberation Day all the hidden airmen from the village appeared in their civilian clothes, all unaware of each other's existence up to that point. Richard distinctly remembered the tanks coming up the street.

We hadn't had a cigarette in all this time, of course, and when they were coming up the street they stopped, and I said 'Have you got any fags?' to this tank feller. He said, 'You speak good English.' I said, 'I bloody well should do. I'm a Scouse!' We got an unlimited supply of cigarettes after that.

From then on all they wanted to do was get back to England, and seven liberated airmen were finally given a truck and went toting around the aero-dromes trying to find a way home. Eventually they found an aerodrome where they were put in a Dakota and flown back to England. Richard was given a fortnight's leave because of his experience, and when he returned he was interviewed by a WAAF officer, who asked him if he was all right, to which he replied, 'Yes, my nerves are shot to pieces of course but basically I am fit.' 'So you can go back flying?' He said, 'Oh yes, but I'm not doing any more bloody ops though.' He told her that he had done his share, the invasion had happened and the war was nearly over. He said he would go to Transport Command and spent his last two years in the RAF flying Stirlings and Yorks with No. 242 Squadron based at RAF Stoney Cross in Hampshire, but which also included lengthy periods in Burma. He was finally demobbed as a Warrant Officer in September 1946.

After the war Richard had no contact with any of the rest of the crew. More than sixty years after the event, he finally returned to the area where he had spent so much time in hiding. 'The village had gone, everything that I remembered had gone. When I think back, I think well, I shouldn't be here today. To be shot down in the first place, to be rescued, to come back and to fly again, it's unbelievable.' ●

Left Richard Wensley, 2006. (*Richard Wensley*)

CHAPTER SEVEN

FROM FIGHTER TO BOMBER COMMAND

SEAN FEAST

THE MEN OF BOMBER COMMAND WERE NOT ALWAYS 'BOMBER BOYS' IN THE 'TRADITIONAL' SENSE. ON 8 NOVEMBER 1943, A NEW SPECIAL DUTIES UNIT – NO. 100 GROUP – WAS FORMED UNDER THE COMMAND OF AIR COMMODORE (LATER AIR VICE MARSHAL) E. B. ADDISON. ITS REMIT WAS TO BRING ALL OF THE ELECTRONIC WARFARE AND RADIO COUNTER MEASURES (RCM) UNITS UNDER A SINGLE COMMAND. IT WAS ALSO RESPONSIBLE FOR THE VARIOUS 'SPOOFING' ELEMENTS, AS WELL AS SEVERAL SQUADRONS OF DE HAVILLAND MOSQUITOES ENGAGED ON INTRUDER OPERATIONS TO HUNT OUT THE GERMAN NIGHTFIGHTER FORCE AND PROTECT THE BOMBER STREAM. BOMBER SUPPORT, AS IT CAME TO BE KNOWN, IS AN INTRINSIC PART OF THE BOMBER COMMAND STORY, AND WITHIN ITS RANKS WERE MEN WHOSE CAREERS WERE AS DIVERSE, AND AS EVENTFUL, AS THE MOST SEASONED BOMBER BARONS.

HARRY WHITMILL WAS born in Acton on 6 November 1919, almost a year to the day after the bloody carnage of the First World War ended. His father – who was also called Harry – had served with distinction in the army, but was eventually invalided out on medical grounds, and struggled to bring up a growing family of six children with only limited means.

Despite such adversity, and with the support of his older sister Ivy, Harry junior did well at school – so well that he gained entry to the local Grammar School. Upon leaving education he qualified as an accountant with Great Western Railways (GWR) and, with war looming, joined the Royal Air Force Volunteer Reserve (RAFVR). Then came the declaration of war, and at 19 the young Harry arrived at Hatfield Elementary Flying Training School to begin a period of some eight months' training. Rated 'average' at the conclusion of the first stage of his training on De Havilland Tiger Moths on 12 December 1940, he progressed to Service Flying Training School at RAF Cranfield to fly twin-engine Airspeed Oxfords. He was once again rated as 'average' on flying the larger aircraft, and in May 1941 was posted to No. 54 Operational Training Unit (OTU) at RAF Church Fenton.

Church Fenton had been home to the first RAF 'Eagle' Squadron during the Battle of Britain and, because of its location away from the front line (north Yorkshire), had been a popular base for battle-weary squadrons to rest and recover. Initially with No. 13 Group, in August 1940 it had been transferred to No. 12 Group, which coincided with a change in role, when it became a dedicated training base for nightfighter aircrew.

Harry spent two months at RAF Church Fenton, primarily flying the Bristol Blenheim, before once more progressing to RAF Debden for a short spell prior to his first operational posting, No. 257 Squadron at RAF Coltishall.

Having flown anti-submarine patrols in the last few months of the First World War, No. 257 'Burma' Squadron had re-formed in May 1940 at RAF Hendon. Initially flying Spitfires before swapping for Hurricanes, the Squadron became operational in July and fought with distinction throughout the Battle of Britain. Among its most noteworthy pilots

Left A formal portrait, not long after receiving his 'wings', December 1940. *(Via Sean Feast)*

were such luminaries as Bob Stanford-Tuck DSO, DFC & two Bars, 'Cowboy' Blatchford DFC and Prosser Hanks DFC – all later wing commanders and all notable fighter pilots and 'aces' of their time.

By the time that Harry arrived in August 1941, the Squadron had moved to RAF Coltishall on the north Norfolk coast and was taking part in sweeps over northern France. Bob Tuck had been promoted to command the Duxford Wing, Prosser Hanks posted to No. 56 Squadron, and 'Cowboy' Blatchford was, for a short while at least, the No. 257 Squadron officer commanding (OC). He would shortly after hand over the reins to acting Squadron Leader Francis Soper DFC, DFM, an established 'ace' in his own right with more than a dozen 'kills' to his name. (Soper had the unusual nickname of 'Marshal Budenny', as his eccentric moustaches were likened to the soviet revolutionary cavalry officer of that name.)

Harry was familiar with the Hurricane, having flown the aircraft at OTU and going solo for the

Flight Sergeant Harry Whitmill (centre) having just shaken hands with the King, probably at RAF High Ercall. Note the distinctive tail fin of one of the unit's Turbinlite Havocs. *(Via Sean Feast)*

first time on the type on 22 June 1941. As part of 'A' Flight under the command of Flight Lieutenant Richard Mason, he now started flying a series of air tests, night-flying practice flights and practice interceptions, before commencing operations that comprised primarily convoy and fighter patrols. A logbook entry for 5 October 1941 states simply: 'Sea search (ops)'. The search was for Squadron Leader Soper, who had been shot down off the Suffolk coast. Sadly their search was in vain.

October proved to be a busy month for the fledgling fighter pilot, an inked swastika in his logbook denoting the destruction of a Dornier 217 during a convoy patrol on 27 October. Beside the swastika and aircraft type, Harry has written 'Sgt Slaney'. John Slaney had joined 257 in July, but this was his first victory. Whether Harry took any part in the combat is not clear, but it was obviously a significant enough event to warrant inclusion in his log.

The Squadron moved from RAF Coltishall to RAF Honiley in November 1941, by which time it was using both the Hurricane IIb and IIc. It moved again in July 1942 to High Ercall in Shropshire, by which stage the Squadron had become one of the first to receive the Hawker Typhoon, and the pilots began low-level patrols in September to intercept Jagdbomber or 'Jabos' – the sneak fighter bomber raids that had become a favourite tactic of the Luftwaffe during that period. Harry flew a Typhoon for the first time on 26 July 1942.

While at RAF High Ercall, the pilots were intrigued by the arrival of an unusual twin-engine aircraft with an equally unusual fitting. They discovered soon after that this was a Turbinlite Flight from which a new Squadron – No. 535 Squadron – would emerge, albeit briefly. Increasingly, Harry had been training for nightfighter operations, and No. 535 Squadron was most certainly a night-fighting unit. Its modus operandi, however, was remarkable by any measure, and to suggest it was even a 'Heath Robinson' invention is perhaps generous in the extreme.

The concept was simple: a powerful 2,700 million candela searchlight was fitted to the nose of an A20 'Havoc' – an American aircraft then being operated in small numbers by the RAF. The Havoc would be guided towards an enemy aircraft by means of both ground radar and its own radar and,

when in range, the Turbinlite would be switched on and the enemy illuminated. Hurricanes flying in company with the Havoc would then have their very own rabbit in the headlights to shoot down.

Six pilots from 257 were posted to 535 while the experiment took place, and such faith was placed in the new technique that five other Turbinlite squadrons were formed to deal with the night-bomber menace. Perhaps not surprisingly, the concept was not a success. Switching on a brilliant searchlight in the dark had the immediate effect of ruining the pilot's most valuable weapon – his night vision – and the only aircraft shot down in the four months that the squadrons were operational was one of our own bombers. By the end of January 1943, all six squadrons had been disbanded.

There was more excitement of a personal nature for Harry while serving at RAF High Ercall, for it was here that he met and fell in love with the girl he would ultimately marry, Joyce. They had first been attracted to one another at a dance and, shortly after, Harry had arranged to call upon her parents in Wellington, where she lived with her mother, father and two siblings. He later recounted to his sister that, when he called at the house, Joyce answered the door in a gymslip. She was 18 and studying at college. Suffice to say an 18-year-old in a dance dress looks considerably more grown up than a teenager in a gymslip, and Harry was temporarily flustered at the thought of being a cradle snatcher!

Harry spent only four weeks with 535 until October 1942, before being posted to yet another new squadron then forming at RAF Northolt, and soon after moving to RAF Heston. By now, Harry's predilection for night flying had been firmly established, and his new unit – No. 515 Squadron – would test his night-fighting skills still further. The Squadron had evolved from a Defiant Flight – the Boulton Paul Defiant being unusual for a single-engine fighter aircraft in having no forward-firing canon or machine guns, but relying instead on a quadruple-barrelled gun turret to the rear of the pilot's cockpit. When the aircraft had first appeared on the scene in daylight, the German fighters had a nasty surprise. Attacking from the rear in the belief that the aircraft were Hurricanes, a good number of enemy aircraft were shot down before the

Left
Harry Whitmill and
Joyce Fryer upon
their engagement.
(Via Sean Feast)

weaknesses of the Defiant were exposed. Later, the Defiants were considered suitable only for night fighting, and in the early winter of 1942 they were equipped with the latest wizardry from the Telecommunications Research Establishment (TRE) and Aeroplane and Armament Experimental Establishment (A&AEE) to jam enemy radar. The secret trials, codenamed Operation Moonshine, continued for several months, with Harry flying more than his fair share of Moonshine patrols. The officer commanding No. 515 Squadron on Harry's arrival was Squadron Leader Samuel Thomas DFC, AFC, a very experienced exponent of the Defiant who had been engaged in operational flying since May 1940. The citation for his DFC in May 1942 (while with No. 264 Squadron) credits him with at least three victories and a share in a fourth.

Notwithstanding Thomas's prowess, successes on Moonshine patrols were few and far between. There was some excitement, however, on the night of 25 February 1943, when Flight Sergeant Armstrong and his air gunner were some 30 miles off the Dutch coast and spotted an aircraft beneath them at 10,000 feet with a light showing. Losing the aircraft in cloud, and with ice building up on the Defiant's wings, the pilot entered a shallow dive, emerging at 6,000 feet, whereupon the same or

another unidentified aircraft was seen above them and to the rear, and made as if to attack. Armstrong took evasive action, turning sharply to port and starboard, with the stalking aircraft following its every move. Sergeant Jordan, the air gunner, opened fire with two short bursts and their would-be assailant broke off the engagement. Although the outcome – and indeed the identity of the other aircraft – was unknown, another returning crew (Flying Officer Sinton and Flight Sergeant Johnson) reported the dropping of flares in the combat area, and the Navy later reported seeing an unidentified aircraft falling into the sea. It was one exciting and eventful trip in an otherwise tedious and deadly dull existence for the Defiant crews.

Operational flying affected the men in different ways and, although Harry did not speak of his experiences, his sister Ivy noticed the strain in his face when they met. Like many pilots at that time, Harry never flew without a lucky mascot, in his case a small white plastic elephant. Ivy remembers Harry calling her one time to say that his mascot was missing, and perhaps he had dropped it in the garden on his last leave: 'I frantically went on my knees,' she wrote, 'looking through the lawn (which needed cutting I remember) and was so pleased when I found [it].'

Flying the Defiant meant that Harry now had crew, or at least an air gunner. His regular gunner was Flight Sergeant Hugh 'Digsy' Moule – so called because he lived off base in Digs. Digsy and Harry became close friends and would spend much of their spare time socializing. But tragedy was to strike early in April. Having spent the morning on an air firing exercise and taking a ten-minute night-flying test in the afternoon, Harry and Digsy set off on patrol, alive to the possibility of finding and destroying a German intruder. They had been stooging around the night sky for more than an hour and a half when they were given a specific course to steer, which, unbeknown to either of them, would take them straight through a barrage balloon defence. Somebody had blundered badly. Before Harry was able to realize what was wrong, there was a sickening scraping of metal upon metal as the Defiant's wing struck a steel cable. The effect was catastrophic. Harry immediately lost control of the aircraft and ordered Digsy to take to his parachute. Digsy hesitated, until Harry shouted at him to get out, at the same time insisting he would not be far behind. Then, just as suddenly as the collision had caught them unawares, the aircraft caught fire. Harry wrenched back the cockpit canopy, unbuckled his safety harness and dropped out, losing one of his flying boots in the process. Harry remembers the parachute cracking open above his head, two swings and then hitting the ground with a thud. Catching his breath, he stood up as a number of men were approaching and reached into his pocket. Assuming he was searching for a cigarette, one of the men offered him a smoke, to which Harry said in true Brylcreem style: 'No thanks I'm looking for my comb!'

Harry was happy and lucky to be alive; he had baled out at around 700 feet, and it was a miracle that his parachute had time to deploy. But his good humour at his own survival was short-lived. Soon after he learned that Digsy was dead. Although he had made it out of the aircraft in one piece, he may have struck his head on the Defiant's tail, as his parachute never opened.

Harry would later act as a pallbearer at his friend's funeral, and lean heavily on Joyce to help him through the shock of Digsy's death and the guilt at his own survival.

Yet another change in aircraft type came in June 1943 when the first Bristol Beaufighters began to arrive and finally replaced the Defiants in December (the Squadron having become non-operational in August). The 'Beau' was a very different beast from the Defiant, although its performance was broadly similar. Both the Defiant II and the Beaufighter II took advantage of the Rolls-Royce Merlin XX, giving them a top speed comfortably in excess of 300mph. Service ceiling was also similarly comparable, but where the Beaufighter really won was in its range. Whereas the Defiant had a range of around 500 miles, the Beaufighter was capable of three times that distance, making it ideal for deeper penetration raids into enemy airspace. Harry was also lucky enough to fly the Beaufighter VI with its two Bristol Hercules VI engines pulling some 1,670 horsepower. This gave it a top speed in excess of 330mph, and with four 20mm cannon in the nose and a further six .303 machine guns in the wings, it packed a fearsome punch.

The change in aircraft also coincided with a change in airfield, the Squadron moving to RAF Hunsdon on the Hertfordshire/Essex border. A new officer commanding was also appointed, Wing Commander James Inkster, and the Squadron settled into flying night-intruder operations.

Change of even greater significance followed towards the end of 1943 with the decision to place all of the various 'special duties' squadrons and 'Bomber Support' units into one group, No. 100 Group, under the leadership of Air Commodore 'Eddie' Addison, with his headquarters at Bylaugh Hall, East Dereham. The responsibility for No. 515 Squadron therefore moved from Fighter to Bomber Command; at a Squadron level, leadership passed to Wing Commander Frederick Lambert (later DSO, DFC) and the Squadron moved again to RAF Little Snoring in Norfolk in December.

There had been changes too in Harry's personal circumstances. In September, notification of his commission had arrived; the former Warrant Officer was now Pilot Officer Henry Whitmill on probation. On 12 February 1944, an even greater event occurred when he and Joyce tied the knot at Wellington Parish Church – a brief respite from war and an opportunity to share with friends their hopes for the future, however long that might be.

Far left Mourners tend the grave of Harry Whitmill. *(Via Sean Feast)*

Left The temporary sign in the foreground reads: 'Here rests two English aviators killed on the field of honour.' *(Via Sean Feast)*

In terms of equipment, by the autumn of 1943, the thoroughly reliable Beaufighter was steadily being phased out in preference for an even greater twin-engine masterpiece that is perhaps synonymous with night-intruder operations – the De Havilland Mosquito. Mosquitoes had been appearing on the Squadron in ones and twos for several months, and Harry got his hands on the controls for the first time in the company of Squadron Leader John Shaw (Shaw would later lose his life on D-Day, 6 June 1944). He did not have the chance to fly solo, however, until 1 March, such that he had only a handful of hours on the type (a Mosquito MkII) by the time the Squadron commenced intruder operations four nights later.

On the morning of 9 April, the Squadron was released until 1200 hours on account of 'the continual night work for the past week' (according to the Operations Record Book), and to give the ground crews a rest. Seven aircraft were detailed for operations that evening. In the late afternoon Harry took one of the Mosquitoes on a night-flying test.

Shortly before midnight, Harry and his 21-year-old navigator, Flying Officer David Biggs, clambered through the bottom hatch of their aircraft, Mosquito NS948, and settled themselves in for their pre-flight checks. The cockpit was cramped, which was both a hindrance and an advantage: a hindrance for it left little room to manoeuvre, especially for the navigator; an advantage, because the proximity of the pilot/navigator allowed for better communication.

Switching on the ignition and pressing both the starter and the booster coil buttons while the ground crews worked the priming pump, Harry listened as the engines quickly burst into life. He then checked the temperatures and the pressures, and that the

various hydraulic-driven surfaces were performing satisfactorily. Taxying around the perimeter track while testing the brakes, Harry and David ran through the checklist for take-off: trimming tabs; propeller; fuel; flaps. With the brakes released, and the engines screaming, Harry kept the Mosquito straight on the runway, countering the tendency for a slight swing to port by opening the port throttle slightly ahead. He raised the tail wheel by a light forward pressure on the control column, and the Mosquito effortlessly climbed into the air. Harry selected the undercarriage 'up' and checked for two green lights. At an Indicated Air Speed (IAS) of 148 knots, the aircraft began to climb. It was a fraction after 2253 hours.

The brief was to patrol the area of Paris/Lille and hunt out enemy fighters. No one knows what happened, beyond that the aircraft failed to return. Both men were originally buried near to where their aircraft fell, between Coulommiers and Solers, and later reinterred in the cemetery at Villeneuve-Saint-Georges. ●

Left Harry Whitmill's grave at Villeneuve-Saint-Georges' Old Communal Cemetery. *(Via Sean Feast)*

CHAPTER EIGHT

THERE WAS STILL
THE THREAT FROM BELOW

STEVE DARLOW

COMMAND OF THE AIR WAS A KEY REQUIREMENT FOR THE SUCCESS OF THE JUNE THROUGH AUGUST 1944 NORMANDY INVASION, THE SECURING OF THE BEACHHEAD AND THE BREAK-OUT INTO OCCUPIED FRANCE. ALLIED AIR SUPERIORITY OVER NORMANDY DURING THE LAND BATTLE WAS SUCH THAT OFTEN THE ROYAL AIR FORCE HEAVY BOMBERS DEEMED IT SAFE TO RETURN TO LARGE-SCALE ATTACKS DURING DAYLIGHT HOURS. OFTEN THE BOMBER BOYS WERE CALLED IN TO BREAK OPEN THE ENEMY GROUND DEFENCES, AS PART OF SIGNIFICANT LAND OFFENSIVES. THE FIGHTER BOYS WOULD BE PROTECTING THE AERIAL FLANKS, WHILE THE BOMBER BOYS TRIED TO BREAK THE STALEMATES. THE THREAT OF ENEMY FIGHTER ATTACKS HAD BEEN GREATLY REDUCED, BUT THE GROUND DEFENCES COULD STILL PROVE DEADLY.

Henry Oakeby volunteered for the air force when the war started. He was working as a jig and tool-maker, a reserved occupation, but eventually he was called up and sent to South Africa to work as a ground engineer and 'for 3 years I was messing around with spanners'. As the Allied air offensive in Europe escalated, and the RAF squadrons began to equip with the four-engine heavy bombers – Avro Lancasters, Handley Page Halifaxes and Short Stirlings – the demand for flight engineers grew rapidly. When news came through to South Africa, Henry was keen to take up flight engineer aircrew duties and tried to sign up numerous times. 'But the Chief Technical Officer stopped us all going – several times. But one particular time he happened to be on leave and we all went.'

Henry came back to England and to RAF St Athan, where he completed a flight engineer course, and in December 1943 he was posted to No. 1679 Conversion Unit – his logbook recording that on 9 January 1944 he qualified as a flight engineer on Lancaster IIs. A posting to Royal Canadian Air Force No. 432 Squadron followed – part of the Canadian No. 6 Group. Henry found himself the only Englishman on the crew, a common feature with respect to flight engineers on the Canadian squadrons.

To say that Henry was thrown in at the deep end is putting it mildly: it was 'a bit of a hair raiser to start with'. His first operation took him to Berlin on the night of 27/28 January 1944, part of a 515 Lancaster and 15 Mosquito attack on the German capital – bombing through cloud cover. A total of thirty-three Lancasters were lost, including that of No. 432 Squadron's Pilot Officer D. Paterson RCAF, with a complete loss of life. A bomb hang-up forced a landing for Henry's crew at RAF Wratting Common and then a return to base the following day, at which point they were able to record the basic facts of what they had seen.

No actual fires could be seen but the glow from the fires could be seen on the way out of the target area. At 1953 hours while flying at 22,000 feet a twin-engined aircraft with a light in the nose came in from port and below but broke away from starboard. The mid-upper gunner and rear gunner fired short bursts with no result.

On the night of 30/31 January Henry returned to the air battle above Berlin, part of a 534-aircraft attack from which 32 Lancasters and 1 Halifax failed to return.

During February new Halifax IIIs arrived at No. 432 squadron, Henry noting qualification on the new type in his logbook on Valentine's Day. Familiarization flights followed, and on 24 February Henry's crew were detailed to be part of the 734 aircraft raid on Schweinfurt's ball-bearing factories. On return from the operation Henry's crew report recorded that 'a heavy bomber was seen going down in flames at 2208 hours', one of the thirty-three aircraft lost on the raid.

Witnessing the shooting-down of other aircraft on a raid brought home, if it needed to be, the perils the bomber crews faced during an operation. Empty spaces at the meal tables back at base and beds not slept in were the immediate realities of a failed to return. But bomber squadrons did not just lose aircraft to enemy action, and No. 432 Squadron was no exception. On 2 February 1944 Flight Sergeant Sieben RCAF lost his life with his entire crew on a training flight – the aircraft, with a damaged engine, crashed into trees on the approach to landing. Then Squadron Leader Strachan DFC, RCAF was killed with his entire crew on a cross-country training flight. The Squadron diary recorded on 22 February: '300 airmen and 25 officers formed at Flight Offices and marched to the funeral of Squadron Leader Strachan DFC.' Strachan with five of his colleagues rests at Harrogate (Stonefall) cemetery. The seventh member of the crew, American 1st Lieutenant Rorke, was buried at the US Military cemetery, Madingley, Cambridge. On 12 April the Squadron suffered yet another fatal training accident, seven of the eight men on board Halifax LW614 QO-S killed owing to engine failure.

Henry's crew's next full operation (they had been forced to turn back from a raid on Stuttgart at the beginning of March) marked a turning point in Bomber Command's air offensive. The forthcoming invasion of Normandy was to become the overriding consideration for all the UK-based Allied forces, and a key requirement for Bomber Command was

Right
Flight Engineer
Henry Oakeby.
(Henry Oakeby)

to attack supply lines to the proposed battle area. This included the destruction of railyards through which German reinforcement would deploy, and the 'Transportation Plan' identified the rail targets deemed necessary for attack. The first strike took place on the night of 6/7 March 1944, when 261 Halifaxes and 6 Mosquitoes were despatched to Trappes. A total of nine 1,000lb and six 500lb bombs fell from Henry's Halifax, adding to the devastation of the railyards.

Two raids to the railyards at Le Mans followed, although on the first bombs were withheld. Then on the night of 18/19 March Henry kept a check on the engines of his Halifax, which was one of a fleet of 846 aircraft that carried out a particularly destructive raid on Frankfurt. The next time Henry Oakeby and his crew were operational, they were detailed to take part in what would prove to be the worst night for Bomber Command in the history of the war. Out of 795 aircraft sent on the raid, 95 bombers and crews were lost – a greater loss of aircrew than were sacrificed by Fighter Command during the entire Battle of Britain. 'It was the longest raid we did.' Take-off was 2200 hours, the Halifax returning to base at 0616 hours. 'We had seen flashes and thought they were scarecrows, but they were aeroplanes being shot down.' At the time it was believed that the Germans were firing 'scarecrow' shells – designed to look like exploding bombers. History now seems to show that they were indeed exploding bombers.

During April two French rail targets and two German targets featured in Henry Oakeby's logbook, and the following month it was exclusively pre-invasion raids, with four raids on railyards, including a 22/23 May attack on Le Mans in which the crew were forced to make two orbits waiting for target markers to appear. The month was completed with the obliteration of an enemy radio installation at Mont Couple. During May No. 432 Squadron lost 5 aircraft on operations; 26 airmen gave their lives, 6 became prisoners and 6 evaded capture.

On 5 June 1944 Henry and his crew were again detailed for operations. Nothing unusual was in the air; it appeared to be just another raid. 'There was no mention at all of invasion – it was nothing

Left Henry Oakeby's logbook for the first week of March 1944 showing his involvement in the historic raid to Trappes on the night of 6/7 March 1944. *(Henry Oakeby)*

special.' They would be attacking the enemy guns at Houlgate, defending the approach to the Normandy beaches. Taking off at 0147 hours, Henry's Halifax headed for Normandy, as below the vast Allied armada approached the beaches. At 0352 hours, from 10,000 feet, seven 1,000lb and six 500lb bombs were dropped on Pathfinder markers, the crew landing back at base at 0619 hours. The Squadron diary reported: 'The great news of the Allied landing this morning was received with great pleasure as the beginning of the end.'

For the rest of June Flight Lieutenant Cooper's crew, apart from one raid on the synthetic oil plant at Sterkrade, found themselves exclusively attacking French targets: railyards and flying bomb launch and storage sites in response to the opening of the German V1 offensive in the middle of the month. Into July, with twenty-four operations already recorded in Henry's logbook, his pilot, Flight Lieutenant Cooper, continued to apply the skills of his aircrew team in the disruption of the V1 launch rates, as they took part in raids on the supply site at Biennais on 4 and 5 July and the storage sites at Thiverny and Nucourt on 12 and 15 July respectively. In between, No. 432 Squadron sent sixteen Halifaxes to blast enemy tank concentrations and

shatter the stalemate around Caen on 7 July; Henry wrote in his logbook: 'Good Prang'. The Squadron diary recorded: 'The following message arrived about an hour before all our aircraft returned. "A heavy bomber attack has just taken place. A wonderful impressive show and enormously appreciated by the Army." The Second Army request that appreciation be sent to all crews.'

On 18 July 1944 the airmen of Bomber Command were once more called in to blast open the Normandy front lines around Caen, as part of the launch of Operation Goodwood. A staggering 667 Lancasters, 260 Halifaxes and 15 Mosquitoes were despatched on the daylight raid to bombard the German positions with over 5,000 tons of explosives. No. 432 Squadron played its part, sending sixteen aircraft, including Halifax VII NP706 QO-J, lifted from the RAF East Moor runway at 0326 hours by Flight Lieutenant Cooper, with Henry Oakeby as his flight engineer. The Squadron diary recorded the task set out for the bomber fleet, 'paving the way for an advance in Normandy by bombing concentrations of tanks and material and obliterating a strong hold on the east side of the river Orne, outside Caen'. Over the target the skies were free of enemy aircraft and, as historians Chris

Left Henry Oakeby's logbook and the details of his July 1944 raids, including the 18 July operation against German positions around Caen. *(Henry Oakeby)*

Everitt and Martin Middlebrook state in *The Bomber Command War* Diaries: 'Allied air superiority over the battlefield by day was complete.' But there was still the threat from below. 'We bombed and were on the turn and then a big bang. "Christ, we've been hit."' Flak had slammed the aircraft midships on the port side, and Henry went back to assess the damage. As flames belched into the fuselage, Henry heard his skipper call that the controls had gone on the port side and that he had no control. 'The skipper said bail out. I was the second to last – the skipper was the last. My big worry was that the ground wasn't coming up quickly enough and I would be shot at. I was coming down so slowly.'

From Henry's crew nearly all managed to survive except the Canadian mid-upper gunner, Robert Elwood Burton, who rests in Bretteville-sur-Laize Canadian War Cemetery.

When I landed I could hear voices. We had been briefed to bury our Mae West and parachute but mine were left hanging, caught in trees. I got my compass out and headed north, coming across the river Orne. I sat for a while and had a cigarette then heard more voices and walked across the river – up to my waist in water. I climbed up on a rock, took off my flying boots and dried off my socks. Coming to the top of the bank I could see a little farmhouse and people through the window – they weren't our people, they must be Germans. I turned and walked away.

Shortly afterwards Henry was approached by 'this little bloke, Edmondé Baretté, who said "Angleterre". I said "yes" and was taken to his uncle, who was living in caves by the Orne.' Henry was welcomed in and a decision was made to keep him where he was and to be given a false identity.

They christened me Fernard Huard – a deaf and dumb farm labourer from Calvados. I also had a brother called André Huard, who could speak English pretty well. After a time he told me he was a German tank commander who had fallen at the battle of Caen. There he met a French family and when he said his mother was French and his father was German, they said 'You're a Frenchman. Stay with us.' So he and I – brothers.

Edmondé Baretté's father used to walk along the river, and often when the Germans went swimming he would take their boots, fill them with stones, and send them to the bottom.

Some Russians, who had been labourers, had some guns and they had a plan to go over the Pyrenees. André wondered if we should go with them. We got out the escape maps and had a look – a bloody long way. So we decided to decide the next day and that's when the tanks arrived.

After about ten days, and because of Allied advances, the Germans moved along all the civilians, including the Huard 'brothers'. For the next three

weeks Henry continued to work as a farm labourer, living in a barn. Then one morning he was woken by rumbling noises. 'I looked out and there were tanks going down the road. I could see khaki uniforms. I was about to rush out but thought that there might still be SS troops about. So I went back to sleep.' A couple of hours later Henry approached one of the tanks.

This bloke came out and he said, 'Do you want to come with us?' I said, 'No fear.' So he told me to go up the road to an armoured car and talk to

Right
RAF St Athan, May 1946. Henry Oakeby is seated at the front third from the left.
(Henry Oakeby)

them. I came across a Group Captain who asked if I smoked. I said, 'I've been smoking dried apple leaves.' He brought me a packet of Players No. 3. I had them up my nose and was giving them to my friends – we were all puffing away. I was taken back to the company HQ by a motorcyclist and told a Captain who I was. We shook hands and he said 'Hey, Cookie. Get us some sandwiches.' Cookie replied, 'Sorry Captain I'm off duty. I've been on all night.' The Captain seemed unsympathetic. 'This guy has been behind enemy lines making it easy for us. Get some

******* sandwiches.' Sandwiches were provided.

Henry was taken back to St Lô by jeep and then to Arromanches to board a Tank Landing Craft for a most unpleasant seasick crossing to Southampton. He was then given a 'new' scruffy uniform and went on leave, following which he was posted to Transport Command.

After the war Henry was able to trace the French people who had assisted him behind the enemy lines, establishing firm friendships. RAF Bomber Command veteran Henry Oakeby died in 2011. ●

CHAPTER NINE

LETTERS HOME

ANDREW MACDONALD

'HE'S JUST A BOY', MY WIFE REMARKED, AS I HANDED HER A SMALL PORTRAIT PHOTO OF AN AIRMAN IN HIS 'BEST-BLUE'. THEY ALL WERE. ONLY OUR FINEST AND YOUNGEST ARE CARTED OFF TO WAR.

AND THEREIN LIES the great tragedy. I thought him a fine-looking young man – not conventionally handsome perhaps, but there was something about him. I tried for some time to find out how young he was and where he had been born by trawling the online genealogy websites, but the young airman refused to give up all his secrets. I found one Arthur B. O'Connor born in Uxbridge near Oxford in June 1919. Was that the man I was looking for? Possibly. I already knew that this young man had died at war a long time ago. A few photos, a box of medals and a small and incomplete collection of letters home are all that remain of a short life full of adventure. His beloved parents, for whom the letters were originally intended, have long gone now; his sister too perhaps, which might explain why these treasured mementos are now in the care of a man entirely unrelated. I have read each letter carefully. Some are short and others profoundly moving, for they tell you so much about the man behind the pen. But all of them are windows to a period in history that is rapidly disappearing from human memory. While there is so much he did not say, Arthur's letters are important to our understanding of this period in history and of course the people who lived through it. He was a perfect example of his generation. He was clever, engaging, witty at times and above all else completely unaware of his courage. The greatest gift that any generation can give is peace, and we have enjoyed nearly seventy years without the prospect of a world conflict. That is precisely why this exceptional young man went to war, and we should never forget that.

Arthur, like so many of his generation, lived an uncomplicated and modest lifestyle. Schooling was of course necessary, but, for the vast majority of children in the 1930s, a trade or an apprenticeship usually awaited them. University required money and influence. We do not really know what ideas Arthur had for his future, but he enjoyed a close bond with his parents. His dad, James, was a stand-up comedian and actor who performed all over the UK under the stage name of Jimmy Bryant. What Jimmy may have lacked in fame, he more than made up for in sheer talent and ability. He made his audiences laugh and, more importantly, forget the war, if only for a few hours. Arthur's mum, Nell,

was very much a part of the theatre and very likely a performer in her own right. Sadly, so little is known about her. She was, however, a source of constant support for her husband and her two children. Arthur's world, then, was rich in theatrics, laughter and travel. What a life it would have been, and this young man was clearly a positive byproduct of it. We are forever left wondering who he might have been if circumstances had been different. The outbreak of the Second World War changed so many lives. By fate, choice or perhaps a mixture of both, he became one of the many tens of thousands of young men who flew and fought in RAF Bomber Command.

Sending and receiving letters provided a lifeline for many young men. Scores of them were away from home for the first time. Even if it was only a page or two to let his mum and dad know he was 'in the pink' and thriving, Arthur wrote as often and whenever he could. Moreover, just to know

Left
Arthur O'Connor's medals.
(Andrew Macdonald)

that Mum and Dad were all right was equally important to him. Letters offered him a chance to escape from the hardships of service life that was so different from his home life. With the constant postings throughout the UK, home was often far away from friends and family. His parents appear to have travelled extensively during the war. Life was more fluid then. James and Nell moved from one concert hall to the next and almost always as part of a big repertory of actors, dancers and singers. The venues were often elegant Victorian music halls, which included the Queen's Theatre in Rhyl, the Royal County Theatre in Bedford and the Harrow Coliseum in London. There may have been a war on, but I think everyone in the family drew so much from this nomadic life of laughter and entertainment. Arthur's RAF career began at the ACRC or Air Crew Reception Centre. Billeted in residential flats, he was living at No. 6, Hall Road, a stone's throw from the famous Lord's cricket ground. A great many servicemen remember this address, though not always with great affection. It

was here that Arthur was hurriedly introduced to the basics of a disciplined life and more specifically to the RAF way of life. He was issued with his kit, a very uncomfortable bed and a plethora of things to polish within an inch of their lives. Add to that marches, drill and hysterical corporals, and it is not surprising that Arthur, like a lot of boys in his predicament, wondered if he had made the right decision.

Thursday 8:30am   *4/112/C.*
                                              C Squadron
                                         London N.W.8

Dear Mam & Dad,

Well here I am at my new abode, and believe me, I'm browned off to the teeth!! Oh mother, is it worth it!!! Brings back memories of my recruiting days — only this time it's a hundred times worse!! Still, I'm on my way — let's hope I can stay the distance.

Arthur survived the screaming corporals, the spit and polish, and the route marches. He knew what he was doing and that it was necessary. It was tough at times, but he was realistic, as his future was going to be every bit as demanding in the weeks and months ahead. His next surviving letter was written from RAF Bridgnorth in Shropshire. In 1943–4, it was home to an Elementary Air Gunnery School, and many thousands of would-be air gunners would have passed through the main gates. At the top of the letter Arthur entered in his service number, 1629028, for the first and only time. It was unique to him. Alongside it is the lowly rank of Aircraftman Second Class. That rank was hopefully a little less of a permanent arrangement. Admittedly, there was nowhere to go for someone demoted or stripped of his rank. But it was a long way to the top. Arthur's time here consisted of many different things. Primarily it was the start of Arthur's training on gunnery and the turret, which would become his cramped and dangerous world. The recruits concentrated on gun harmonization, turret elevation and trajectory. Arthur would have become acquainted with the names of Boulton Paul and Fraser Nash. They were the two major manufacturers of armament and protection for the bomber planes then in service. Brief images or silhouettes of enemy aircraft would dart across

Right Artie in his 'Best Blue'. *(Andrew Macdonald)*

rooms crowded with young airmen and then disappear. Keen young eyes and guns would work in harmony with one another and follow them quickly. This was an instinct their trainers were looking for and the one skill a gunner could not do without.

Finding a crew, or 'crewing up' as it is often remembered, was a relaxed if haphazard arrangement. It was odd because the Air Force was built on discipline and tradition. Times change, though. In March of 1944, Arthur was posted to RAF Finningley in south Yorkshire, and it was here that he would meet the men who would become so vital to his life. We will never know who chose whom or what it was that each man looked for in a comrade. It began, of course, as a necessary working relationship, but in the days and weeks that followed they soon became close friends. They really did not know all that much about one another to begin with, but, for some unaccountable reason, the process almost always worked to everyone's advantage. Their pilot or 'skipper' was a young trainee architect from a pretty little country town called Gumeracha in South Australia. His name was Howard Cornish and he was 22 years old. The bomb aimer was Terrence Wigg from Chelmsford in Essex. He was probably the eldest at the ripe old age of 23! The crew's navigator and the youngest member was Richard Askie. He was a tender 20 years old and remarkably already married with a young son. Another Australian, Wireless Operator Mervyn Pask, hailed from Townsville in Queensland. All the way down the very back of the bomber, in the most isolated position, sat Arthur. He was the rear gunner. Since there was no mid-upper turret on the Wellington bomber, Irishman 'Paddy' Marsh, the crew's other resident gunner, would have taken turns with Arthur to man the rear turret and protect their crew. And there they were. Six vastly different and very young men were about to embark on the most exciting and potentially dangerous chapter of their lives.

Arthur's training at Finningley began in earnest on 14 March 1944. All six men and an instructing pilot set off for a familiarization flight of two hours and twenty minutes in daylight, known universally as 'circuits and bumps'. The boys, particularly

Left Arthur's crew at Heavy Conversion Unit. Standing left to right: Sergeant Terry Wigg (RAF); Sergeant Arthur O'Connor (RAF); Sergeant "Paddy" Marsh (RAF); Sergeant Richard Askie (RAF); Flying Officer Howard Cornish (RAAF); Sergeant Len James (RAF); Sergeant Mervyn Pask (RAAF). (Andrew Macdonald)

Howard, would have had their first proper chance to get to grips with the fundamentals of a twin-engine bomber in flight and would have circled the airfield in anticipation of the first of many such landings in a variety of different circumstances. The training was now gathering momentum, and within just two days the crew flew their first solo flight together. Off they went again the following day, only this time attempting a landing without the use of flaps. And so it continued. Every single day was spent up in the air, so that the crew could fine-tune their individual skills and gel together as a fighting unit. In addition to frequent cross-country trips, the crew carried out high-level bombing exercises, and Arthur and Paddy would have had the chance to squeeze into the rear turret and fire their four .303 machine guns on air-to-air firing exercises. It was tough work. The hours were long and the training a strain. The days often blended into one another. Howard wrote home to his sister: 'It is Sunday once again but this means nothing as far as work is concerned for me so I can only write a few lines at lunch time.' Arthur too kept a calendar with him, just so that he could check which day of the week it was. That might explain why he never dates his letters.

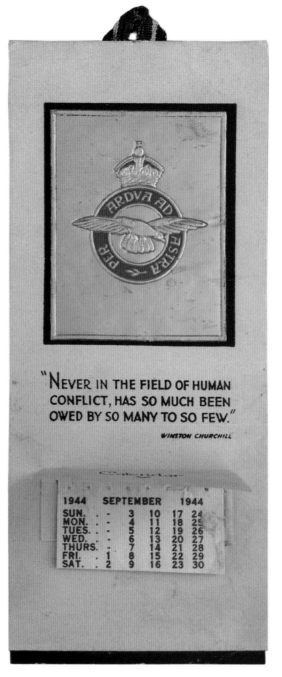

"NEVER IN THE FIELD OF HUMAN CONFLICT, HAS SO MUCH BEEN OWED BY SO MANY TO SO FEW."

WINSTON CHURCHILL

1944	SEPTEMBER				1944
SUN.	.	-	3	10	17 24
MON.	.	-	4	11	18 25
TUES.	.	-	5	12	19 26
WED.	.	-	6	13	20 27
THURS.		-	7	14	21 28
FRI.	.	1	8	15	22 29
SAT.	.	2	9	16	23 30

of the Wellington's belly, the crew threw thousands of propaganda leaflets out into the night sky. They were called 'nickel' raids and, though they were unlikely to have had any long-lasting effect on the people down below, it gave the boys their first taste of what it meant to fly in combat. It may have been passed off as a soft target, but many brave young men were lost on similar sorties, long before they reached an operational squadron and experienced the harsh realities of the bombing campaign. Arthur and crew came home safely after a flight of six hours and thirty-five minutes and no doubt patted themselves on their tired backs for a job well done. They were well on their way now and, although they could not brag about being seasoned aircrew, they had taken their first flight into an uncertain world.

On 7 June 1944, the crew had moved yet again to RAF Blyton in Lincolnshire. At that time, No. 1662 Heavy Conversion Unit was based there and it continued to operate from the airfield until the end of the war. Only a day or so earlier and a few hundred miles to the south of them, thousands of Allied infantrymen had poured ashore at Normandy and fought their way across the French countryside. It was such an extraordinary time to be alive. For Artie, though, the action was far away and the pace of his war was so sedate at times that he must have wondered if indeed there was one.

Tuesday   *Sergeant's Mess.*
Blyton
Nr. Gainsborough
Lincs

Dear Mam & Dad,

I've just finished work, had tea, and here I am in the hut, writing a few lines before getting ready to go out with the lads into Gainsborough. The weather here is smashing – all round the huts the lads are lying about in the 'rude' tanning themselves. Every now and then someone lets out a yell because one of the crew has thrown a bucket of cold water over him!

It was one of those rare blissful moments where everything seemed so peaceful. The boys stretched out in the grass basking in the balmy English sun-shine and fooling around. It was a special moment but a fleeting one. For the next three weeks, the

By April, the boys were flying almost entirely at night, and the flights were becoming progressively longer in duration. The training was gathering momentum. Howard recorded another cross-country exercise in his logbook and it lasted over six exhausting hours before they finally touched down at Finningley in the dead of night. Ten days later, on 21 April, Arthur and his crew flew for the first time over occupied Europe. This was it. Their mission was to fly across the Channel to Dreux in northern France, but, instead of bombs spilling out crew, now joined by their seventh and final member, Flight Engineer Sergeant Len James, applied what they had already learned on Wellingtons to the heavy four-engine bombers that were the mainstay of Bomber Command. In this case, it was the Handley Page Halifax. At some point during their stay at Blyton an unknown photographer captured the crew in full kit standing beneath the imposing presence of a Halifax MkV. It is a magnificent photo and probably the only time all seven of them were photographed together as a crew. By the time they had completed their conversion training in late June, they had accumulated approximately thirty hours in the air during a dozen or so flights. A brief check ride of about forty minutes with an instructor, and the boys were cleared to take the next step in becoming a bomber crew. Artie wrote home to let his parents know that he was on the move once again and that his new address would be RAF Ingham. He would remain there for the next ten days on a bomber defence-training course.

He did not wait long to write home. The very day he arrived at Ingham, Arthur scribbled his thoughts down on some paper. Clearly Ingham did not appeal:

Thursday   _Sergeants' Mess._
                          R.A.F. Ingham
                          Near Lincoln

Dear Mam & Dad,

I arrived here today, and already I am beginning to look forward to the day when the bus will come and collect my kit, and myself and take me away from this. The food (if you call it that) is shocking and I wouldn't even feed a pig in the dining hall!! The impression given on the camp is that we are fighting this war, not for our own personal reasons, but for the benefit of the R.A.F. and all its 'Big Wigs'. And they tell us to smarten ourselves up – well if we are to be treated like pigs, we might as well look like them too!! Thank goodness I am only here ten days. I don't know whether it is the Irish in me but it doesn't take me long to lose my temper!! But they say things are different when you get on 'ops' – believe me, they had better be!!

Well, I'm looking forward to a letter from you tomorrow. It's the only thing that keeps body and soul together in this racket – for me it does anyhow. Well folk, I haven't given you much news but I haven't anything interesting to tell as yet – maybe my next letter will bring forth more fruits! The main thing is – I'm in the best of health.

Arthur closed his letter as he always did with his love and blessings for Mum and Dad. Ten days later, his rant over and his Irish blood no longer on the boil, Arthur happily left Ingham behind him. It was already early July, and the boys were now nearing the end of their flying training. Since the crew were part of No. 1 Group, which operated Lancasters exclusively, it was necessary for them to spend a week or so learning to operate a new machine with its own individual handling characteristics. It is likely they were then sent to RAF Lindholme in south Yorkshire, which in mid-1944 was home to No. 1 Lancaster Finishing School. A handful of Arthur's letters from his stay survive, but as always he tells his parents precious little about what he was doing there. 'What do we do here all day? Oh! Just laze about – good job too as the food's lousy and we just about manage to hang on to some strength!'

The food was always a bone of contention. Nobody liked it, but England was still effectively a besieged country and rationing was an accepted part of life for everyone, regardless of whether you were in the military or a civilian. Arthur picked up a cold while at Lindholme and was admitted to the Squadron sick bay. Right alongside him in the next bed was his 'pal' Richard and the two whiled away the time by 'laughing and joking all day – the both of us make a good Hope–Crosby team!' Fun though it was, their stay had separated them from the rest of the crew, who had already left for RAF Sandtoft. Arthur was increasingly worried about being left behind, but both were relieved to be discharged, and they managed to catch up with the rest of them and complete the last few hours of their Lancaster training.

At long last, after what must have felt like an eternity of postings and courses, the boys arrived by truck at RAF Kelstern on 14 July 1944. The names of all seven are neatly typed into the official personnel movements for No. 625 Squadron. They were now finally at the business end of the Allied bombing offensive over Europe. The invasion of Normandy was a matter of weeks old, and Bomber Command's operational focus had shifted accordingly in support of the landings. Within just four days of their arrival, Arthur and crew were on the Battle Order. Eighteen of the Squadron's Lancasters were bombed up ready to fly an early morning sortie to Sannerville in Normandy. It was a custom within the Squadron for new crews to participate on their first operation with three experienced men beside them. The three selected were considered to be the most essential individuals required greatly to improve the chances of a successful mission and a safe return. The pilot would command the aircraft and watch over the second pilot occupying the engineer's fold-down seat beside him. Then the navigator would guide the aircraft and crew to their target and then back home again. An experienced rear gunner would, it was hoped, provide the crew with sufficient protection either to avoid aerial combat or to bring down a persistent enemy fighter.

The theory worked this time round, and all eight men returned from a successful mission to destroy German fortified positions threatening the Allied advance. Artie had chalked up his first 'trip' as a mid-upper gunner and was no doubt relieved to get back home again and meet up with the two boys they had left behind, Paddy and Richard. With the operational introductions out of the way, the entire crew set off once again on 20 July to bomb a V2 rocket site at Wizernes in France. The operational diary records the crew's participation. In the details column, it says very simply: 'Target bombed at 21:04 hours from a height of 12,500 feet on red and yellow TIs.' Nothing else of note is mentioned, and the operational summary records the sortie as being 'very accurate'. That was it. Surely the raid had left a greater impression on the boys. What were their thoughts and how did they feel afterward? Not surprisingly Arthur never mentions any of his operations to his mum and dad. He clearly did not want to worry them. If he was scheduled to fly, he was 'on duty'. It was as simple as that. There is no mention of the drama that was almost certainly a regular part of his life. It is only after talking to the survivors that you realize how dangerous and nerve-racking it really was. Merv Pask remembers his constant fear of the German flak. On one mission, he drew the curtain across his tiny window in an attempt to reduce the risk of being hit. He laughs when he thinks of it now, but then such a silly reaction, he reasoned, offered him some protection from the hell being unleashed outside. On another daylight mission, Terry Wigg was as always lying on his belly in the bomb aimer's compartment map reading when a fist-sized fragment of anti-aircraft shell ripped its way through the thin fuselage, burnt a hole through his map and narrowly missed leaving a similar-sized hole in his head. That was their life and it was Arthur's too. They shared it together.

As the days and weeks passed, the crew's professional relationship and mutual trust in one another inevitably grew, as it had to. Their very lives depended on it. But some friendships were much stronger than others. Richard was probably Arthur's closest friend. The two of them often shared the brief moments of freedom they had by cycling across the Lincolnshire countryside and visiting the countless villages close by. Howard, in spite of his youth, was acutely aware of his responsibilities, not only to himself but also to the men in his crew. Although they shared the same rank, he was ultimately the decision-maker, and the others knew it. Arthur clearly admired and respected his skipper, but sometimes he did so begrudgingly:

On the subject of leave, the skipper broke the news to his crew today that it's more than likely that our leave will be put back another week. This was immediately followed by passionate outbursts of protest from the crew – in vain, but never-the-less effective to the extent of relieving their feelings! The skipper remained impassive. ('Anybody got a gun!?')

There were other less violent ways of letting off a little steam and it almost always involved a pub, leave or both. Since leave was a long time coming on an operational squadron, the boys would often venture into their local village in search of some liquid refreshment. In a letter to sister, Hazel, Arthur explains how these breaks from reality steadied their nerves and reminded them that they were after all just young men. Some of them were barely out of their teens.

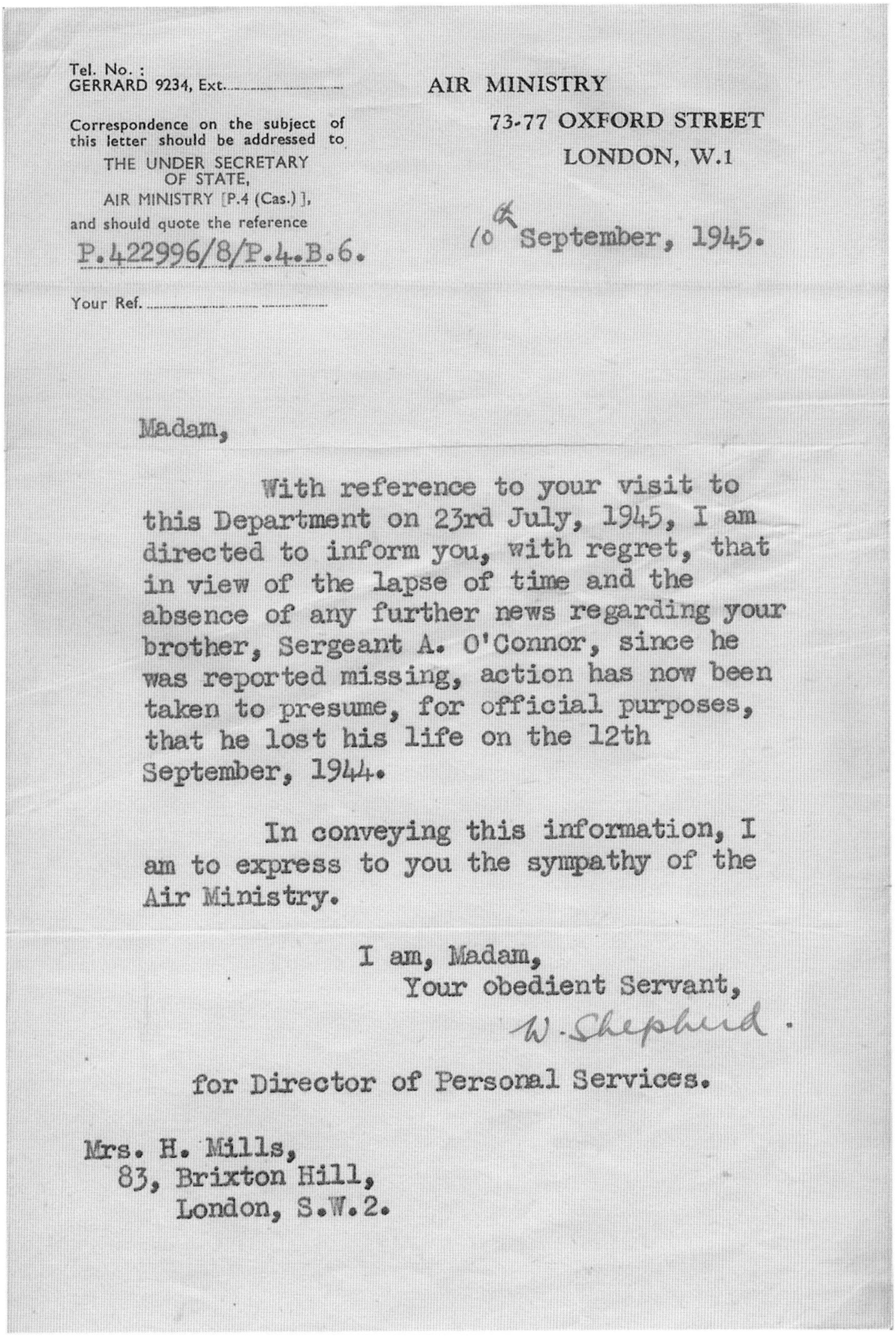

Left Air Ministry
letter to Arthur's sister
– Mrs Hazel Mills.
(Andrew Macdonald)

Tel. No. :
GERRARD 9234, Ext.............................

Correspondence on the subject of
this letter should be addressed to
THE UNDER SECRETARY
OF STATE,
AIR MINISTRY [P.4 (Cas.)],
and should quote the reference

<u>P.422996/8/P.4.B.6.</u>

Your Ref. ....

AIR MINISTRY

73-77 OXFORD STREET

LONDON, W.1

10ᵗʰ September, 1945.

Madam,

      With reference to your visit to
this Department on 23rd July, 1945, I am
directed to inform you, with regret, that
in view of the lapse of time and the
absence of any further news regarding your
brother, Sergeant A. O'Connor, since he
was reported missing, action has now been
taken to presume, for official purposes,
that he lost his life on the 12th
September, 1944.

      In conveying this information, I
am to express to you the sympathy of the
Air Ministry.

      I am, Madam,
        Your obedient Servant,

         W. Shepherd.

      for Director of Personal Services.

Mrs. H. Mills,
  83, Brixton Hill,
    London, S.W.2.

Sessenheim
Communal cemetery.
*(Commonwealth War
Graves Commission)*

Now and again I manage to visit Grimsby, or failing that, Louth, which is a village nearly. It's big enough to be called a town, has two picture halls, a small shopping centre, and of course, a 'pub' on every corner, which, as you may know, is the chief source of entertainment for aircrew! We can't blow our troubles away at 20,000 ft so we try to drown them away at ground level!

Living in such close proximity to all the things that mattered to them had an unusual effect on the men of Bomber Command. The airfields that became their homes had transformed the English landscape, and the people and places they sought to protect were right there beside them. Merv Pask remembered how strange life was for all of them. 'It was a weird, weird life we were leading at the time because you'd be down the pub one night and a few hours later, you could be dead over Germany.'

By the end of July and in just ten days Arthur and the boys had flown five trips. By the end of August that number had reached eleven, and the month came to a close with an epic voyage across northern Germany to the Baltic city of Stettin. After nearly nine hours in the air, the boys and their Lancaster 'E' Easy finally touched down at RAF Kelstern. By the time the boys had collapsed in their beds, the sun was already beginning to rise. Between 5 and 10 September, Bomber Command pounded the port of Le Havre, and Artie flew on all four raids with his crew. Within hours of the bombardment, and before the dust and smoke had had time to settle, two British infantry divisions advanced on the port, and the German garrison there subsequently surrendered. On 12 September, the names of 136 young men appeared on the Battle Order of No. 625 Squadron. Arthur's was one of them. Throughout the day RAF Kelstern was buzzing with activity, as every available soul there prepared for a 'maximum effort' on the city of Frankfurt. There was nothing particularly ominous about this raid, unless, of course, you were superstitious or a born fatalist. Most men possessed a measure of the two just to keep going. Arthur, though, was a wise young lad, so the fact that he was unofficially flying on his thirteenth sortie would

probably not have bothered him as much as leaving four of their crew behind. They knew what this meant. The Lancaster too was an old bird and unfamiliar to them, but if she had survived five months of continual combat, then perhaps that was a good omen. It depended entirely on your point of view.

At 6:15pm Squadron Leader Hamilton, ably assisted by his flight engineer, pushed the throttles forward, and the Lancaster thundered down the main runway. Every minute or so another would follow, until finally all nineteen Lancasters were airborne. Arthur and his crew were among the last to leave. Under strict radio silence and at low altitude, the crew of Lancaster LM512 crossed the coast of Belgium and flew deep into France on a south-easterly course. They were nearing the border between Germany and Alsace. The River Rhine below them shimmered in the light of the moon. At about eight o'clock in the evening they reached their final turning point before their run into Frankfurt. Howard turned the control column, and the Lancaster banked to the left. It was probably at this point that the unthinkable happened. Two heavily laden Lancasters collided with one another at high speed. In a heartbeat, Artie and his crew were gone. Eyewitnesses in the village of Sessenheim far below heard 'an indescribably violent explosion' that lit up the night sky. In the seconds that followed, the wreckage of the two broken bombers cascaded to the ground and covered approximately 2 square miles of the surrounding countryside. There were no survivors from either crew. Even at this chaotic period of the war, the German police and local authorities were still efficient enough to cordon off the main crash sites from the usual souvenir hunters and curious onlookers. The remains of fourteen airmen were discovered among what wreckage remained, and they were almost immediately buried in the local village cemetery at Sessenheim. Very sadly, it seems, little respect was observed at the time, and the fourteen young lads were unceremoniously thrown into a large open grave and buried. The local people were expressly forbidden from participating, but, despite the best efforts of the Germans to stop them, they defiantly turned up in great numbers and left flowers for their fallen heroes.

The battle for Europe continued, and the Western Allies pushed their way across France towards the borders of Germany. Once again the war returned to Sessenheim, and any records positively identifying the young fliers were lost with the destruction of the Town Hall in the intense fighting that followed. More than a year after Arthur's disappearance, sister Hazel was still pressing the authorities for information. Arthur's family must have known the inevitable, but, as he was still officially unidentified, there was some chance at least. As each day passed, though, any hope of Artie's safe return began to fade. In May of 1947 a Flying Officer R. A. Edgar of the Missing Research and Enquiry Unit returned to the scene of the crash in an attempt to ascertain exactly what had happened and positively to identify the two crews buried in a communal grave. The wreckage had long gone, and the surrounding fields bore no visible scars of that horrible night in September 1944. Interviews were conducted with two principal witnesses, but there was little they could add to what had simply been a very tragic mid-air accident in war. The worst was yet to come, as the single grave was opened up, and the boys exhumed one final time. At least now they would be afforded the dignity they so rightly deserved, but it would not have been an easy assignment for the teams involved. They really were incredibly dedicated people, and popular history appears to have forgotten them.

Fifteen airmen now rest side by side in a small village cemetery they helped to liberate nearly seventy years ago. They are among friends now and are at peace. Howard lies in grave number 5. Richard rests a little further down in grave number 10. Little Artie, the boy whose tattered letters helped to inspire this story, is almost certainly in grave number 14, but we cannot be sure. The remaining four men left behind on 12 September 1944 remarkably survived the war, although they never flew together again. Terry Wigg continued to fly operationally until he had reached the required number of operations to complete his tour. After the war, he returned home to his native Chelmsford, married in 1952 and welcomed three boys into the world. He passed away in 1994. Len James flew a mission or two and then disappeared from the operations records altogether. He died late in 1990.

He was 69 years old. Paddy Marsh crewed up with another Australian skipper, Robert Pattison and both completed their tour together in November 1944. Paddy then promptly disappeared and no further trace of him has been found. Merv Pask went on to enjoy an astonishing service career with both the RAF and RAAF. At a loose end and narrowly avoiding two very close calls with death, he was invited to join No. 617 Squadron and continued to fly operationally up until the very end of the war. He is well and truly retired now in his 89th year and he lives a quiet and contented life at home in Australia. Old age is a curse certainly, but

The Under-Secretary of State for Air presents his compliments and by Command of the Air Council has the honour to transmit the enclosed Awards granted for service in the war of 1939-45. The Council share your sorrow that SERGEANT A. B. O'CONNOR in respect of whose service these Awards are granted did not live to receive them.

Merv and men like him are only too happy to tell you how lucky they are to have had such full lives, when others like young Artie did not. As he wrote to his sister, Hazel, on her marriage to George Mills:

Although we didn't have the port to go with the cake, the crew 'ate' to your happiness, wished you and George all the very best that life can bring, and hoped (this was my toast) that your children would find a safer and more peaceful world to live in than we had the misfortune to have been brought into. One never knows – I might even see that day myself! ●

CHAPTER TEN

FINDING PETER

ON A WALL IN MY GRANDFATHER'S OFFICE WAS A PHOTOGRAPH OF ONE OF HIS FOUR BROTHERS: PETER. IT SHOWED A YOUNG MAN IN RAF UNIFORM, WITH THE DISTINCTIVE WHITE FLASH IN HIS FORAGE CAP TO DENOTE AIRCREW UNDER TRAINING. THE BROAD SMILE IS INFECTIOUS – THE OPTIMISM OF YOUTH; THE LOVE OF LIFE. WHO HE WAS, WHAT HE DID AND HOW HE DIED WERE NEVER DISCUSSED. HIS PASSING WAS TOO PAINFUL. SOME YEARS AGO I PIECED TOGETHER HIS OPERATIONAL CAREER; WHAT WAS ALWAYS MISSING, HOWEVER, WAS SOMETHING MORE ABOUT THE MAN: HIS CHARACTER; HIS PERSONALITY. THEN, WITH THE DEATH OF THE LAST SURVIVING BROTHER IN 2011, PETER'S DIARY AND LETTERS WERE DISCOVERED. THE STORY OF THE MAN BEHIND THE PHOTOGRAPH CAN AT LAST BE TOLD.

THE FORCE THAT took off to attack Essen on the night of 12 December 1944 comprised 540 aircraft, including 349 Lancasters, 163 Halifaxes and 28 Mosquitoes from Nos 1, 4 and 8 Groups. It was the last heavy night attack by Bomber Command on the city. Albert Speer, Hitler's armament minister, remarked upon the accuracy of the raid in his post-war interrogation. A report from Essen showed that, besides the industrial damage that had been caused, nearly 700 houses were destroyed and a further 1,400 seriously damaged. Civilian casualties were comparatively light, and so too the losses to the RAF. Six Lancasters were missing, one of them the No. 150 Squadron aircraft in which Flight Sergeant C. A. P. Noble – Peter – was the air bomber.

Peter's journey to that final trip over the night skies of the German industrial heartland followed the typical pattern of the time. He was passed as medically fit for active service on Christmas Eve 1941, and the aircrew selection board recommended he train as a pilot. After leaving No. 9 Initial Training Wing (ITW) fitter than he had ever been in his whole life, and passing yet another medical, he reported to No. 7 Elementary Flying Training School (EFTS) near Heaton Park, having been promoted from a humble aircraft hand (A/CH) to leading aircraftman (LAC).

Peter took his first flight on 24 September 1942, in the ubiquitous DH82 Tiger Moth under the tutelage of a Pilot Officer Laws. He flew virtually every day for the next seven days, until, after twelve hours' dual instruction, he took a final flight with Flying Officer Vaughan. The news was not good. Peter had not demonstrated the necessary aptitude as a pilot and, like thousands before him – and thousands after – he was remustered for training as an air bomber. Rather than continue his training under the leaden skies of the Lancashire countryside, however, he was to enjoy the sunnier climes of South Africa.

Very early in the war a decision had been taken to create what became the Empire Air Training Scheme – an ingenious initiative that enabled the training of Commonwealth aircrews overseas. Under the terms of the scheme, the UK supplied nearly all of the aircraft and the nucleus of skilled men, and the Dominions met all other requirements. But it was also necessary to find training space for the RAF's own men. Here, Southern Rhodesia led the way by agreeing to accommodate, administer and partially pay for three Service Flying Training Schools staffed and run primarily for the RAF. Hard on its heels, South Africa offered a share of its expanding training organizations to RAF pupils.

Peter embarked for South Africa – one of 16,857 aircrew to do so during the war – on 18 January 1943, arriving on 26 February after a passage of more than five weeks across a route designed to present the minimum threat from U-boat attack. It was a rough voyage in convoy with three other troopships, and conditions on board with the heat and overcrowding were at times unbearable. The boredom was punctuated by afternoon lectures and the 'usual' ceremony when crossing the equator,

Below Peter Noble, with the 'white flash' in his forage cap to denote aircrew under training. *(Sean Feast)*

No. 9 Initial Training
Wing. *(Sean Feast)*

challenging Neptune for the right to enter his kingdom. Several officers were shaved and ducked, to the amusement of many.

Docking at Durban on the afternoon of 25 February, the men were greeted by a lady on the jetty singing 'Land of Hope and Glory' and 'The White Cliffs of Dover'. Two days later, Peter arrived at No. 41 Air School at Collondale, East London. He was not impressed, and wrote to his father accordingly: 'East London seemed fine when we first arrived (anything would after the ship) but now

improvement on his flying skills: he passed No. 11 Air Bomber course with a 72 per cent average, and bettered the score in the second half of his training with 74 per cent. He impressed his peers sufficiently to be promoted to sergeant.

Air bomber training, even in the benign skies above the South African veldt, was still not without its dangers, and the death of one of his friends clearly impacted on Peter's nerves. A letter dated 29 July 1943 illustrates his feelings at the time: 'One of our chaps was killed in an accident last night. It

Right Peter with two close admirers. 'Kit' is on the right. *(Sean Feast)*

I am seeing things in perspective: it is about 50 years behind the times and governed by the Dutch Reformed Church. On Sunday, for example, no cinemas are open. The YMCA and canteens do their best, but that is totally inadequate.'

Training kept him busy, however, and consisted primarily of dropping high-level and low-level bombs, 11.5lb practice bombs, and gunnery using the Vickers gas-operated machine gun, all carried out in the Airspeed Oxford. For map reading and reconnaissance, the Avro Anson was preferred. Peter's aptitude to air bombing appeared an

seems hard to believe he is dead – he was tremendously popular with the lads. I feel it very badly as he and I were quite good friends – he slept in the next bed to me. Tomorrow we form the escort at his funeral...'

By the end of August, Peter's South African adventure had come to an end, and within days he was on a ship bound for the UK, arriving home on 16 September. He was pleased to be home, and thrilled to be reunited with his girlfriend Irene. After a period of leave, he was posted to No. 6 (O)

AFU – an Advanced Flying Unit whose operations were split between RAF Staverton and RAF Moreton Valence. AFU was an intermediate stage before the Operational Training Unit (OTU). Peter has little to say about his time at Staverton, although he did make mention of a near riot in the cookhouse regarding the quality of the food. His diary entry for 5 January 1944 reads simply: 'Cookhouse staff are going to be purged if we have anything to do with it!'

On 11 January he moved to Moreton Valence, but spent the first few days grounded with an ear infection and, when the inflammation failed to subside, he was obliged to see an ear, nose and throat (ENT) specialist. This proved quite a concern, as he was forced to be put back a course and stay longer at AFU than he would have wished. Indeed, he was not cleared to fly again until the beginning of February, but he endeavoured to keep his spirits up in the meantime by watching a succession of films and helping in the plotting office. He was also introduced to peanut butter, maple syrup and shooting crap – all courtesy of a group of French Canadians in his hut. It must have been incredibly frustrating, however, to see his 'mob' – as he describes them – moving on. His diary entry for 6 February reads

dolefully: '104 are being posted without me to OTU.'

In the end, Peter did not have long to wait, and on 15 February received orders to report to No. 28 OTU at RAF Wymeswold, arriving at 2100 hours that evening. It was at Wymeswold that Peter would at last become part of a 'crew', but before then he was first obliged to spend more time in the classroom, passing a new series of exams on the MkXIV bombsight with an 82 per cent average. He managed to go home on a 48-hour pass, but a cryptic note suggests his leave was 'not a success'. This is clarified by a 'memo to self' from the following week that explains that his relationship with Irene was 'on the rocks'.

Peter resumed flying again at RAF Castle Donington (still part of No. 28 OTU) in March, by which time he had 'crewed up'. Crewing up was a haphazard affair, where the men were left in a hangar and told to sort it out among themselves. It was surprisingly effective and by the end of the session Peter had been joined by a pilot, navigator, wireless operator and two air gunners, and on 16 March they flew as a crew for the first time: 'First trip in a Wimpey (a Vickers Wellington),' he wrote. 'Quite good but shocked a bit by the crash in the evening.'

A fortnight later, however, there was yet another setback. Although it is not exactly clear what prompted the decision, the crew's first 'skipper' said that he could not continue, and the following week was posted. The new boys, therefore, found themselves without a leader, albeit temporarily. Within a fortnight, and now back at RAF Wymeswold, they were introduced to their new pilot – George Devereau – and the relief was palpable. George was from Kent, quite a bit older than the rest of them and married. He was precisely the steady hand that Peter and the rest of the crew needed at that time, and there is clear relief and delight also in Peter's diary entry for 11 April: 'George went solo – hooray! Wellington

left Peter Noble and 'Kit'. Two young lives shattered by war. *(Sean Feast)*

left George Devereau, described by his air bomber as 'a damned fine pilot'. *(Sean Feast)*

Xs. Good kites.' And later: 'George is a damned good pilot.'

Dinghy drill, gunnery flights and bombing practice were followed by a nickel trip on 2 June for which the crew was highly commended. Peter wrote to his father:

We are developing into what is known as a 'gen' crew. Bill Cross, I have been told, is one of the best navigators that has been here – Bill Horlor is a grade one wireless op – George is a damned fine pilot, and the two gunners (Geoff Mills and John 'Mac' Macnamara) came first and second on their course. As a crew we have an 'above average' rating.

With their operational training on two engines coming to a close, George and Mac headed for the Heavy Conversion Unit at RAF Sandtoft (nicknamed 'Prangtoft' on account of the large number of accidents) on 20 June, and the rest of the crew followed twenty-four hours later. Yet more exams were complemented by further flying training, for which the crew was joined by the final member of their group, a flight engineer by the name of Stephen Ward. At 39, Steve was even older than the skipper, and well above the average age for

aircrew. He had been a butcher in civilian life in Clapham, and coveted Peter's pipe and tobacco!

Taking their first flight in a Halifax on 10 July, within a week they were posted to No. 1 Lancaster Finishing School – the final part of a training journey that had taken Peter more than two and a half years to complete. He had been assessed at Sandtoft as being an above average air bomber. On 11 August Peter wrote simply: 'Received joyous news of posting to our Squadron. 550 at North Killingholme. Cor!'

The No. 550 Squadron at which Peter and the crew arrived, on 12 August 1944, had been formed at Grimsby on 25 November 1943 from 'C' Flight of No. 100 Squadron. It had moved to RAF North Killingholme at the beginning of 1944, and at the time of Peter's arrival was under the command of Wing Commander Alan Sisley. Sisley, an Australian, was far from popular, but the same cannot be said for Peter's flight commander, Squadron Leader Arthur Gainsford. Gainsford, a New Zealander, already held the Distinguished Flying Cross (DFC) and Air Force Cross (AFC) for bravery in the air, and would later add the Distinguished Service Order (DSO) for leadership.

As was customary, George Devereau was the

 **Right** The Devereau crew at OTU. Peter is far left and his skipper far right. *(Sean Feast)*

Left Bombing photograph, Agenville, 31 August 1944. *(Sean Feast)*

Bombing photograph, Gilze-Rijen, 3 September 1944. *(Sean Feast)*

shouting to his skipper to execute a corkscrew starboard (a 'cork-screw' was the standard evasive manœuvre). As the enemy aircraft broke away to port, he came into the sights of the mid-upper gunner, Geoff Mills, who also fired off a burst. The Messerschmitt crept away at a very slow speed and appeared to be in difficulties. Although both gunners believed they had hit their target, neither put in a claim. It had been a lucky escape for all concerned.

After the excitement of Stettin, the crew enjoyed a successful daylight trip to Agenville on 31 August, Peter reporting 'good bombing' after the event. He also wrote 'no opposition', which is interesting given that the Squadron lost its officer commanding, who was flying with the crew of a young New Zealand pilot, Pilot Officer Peter Siddall. Sisley, Siddall and six others were killed.

Any suggestion that the bomber crews later in the war had it easy is not always borne out by Peter's descriptions of operations, both in the diary and in his letters home:

September 3. Gilze Rijen airfield. Holland. Bloody good prang. None lost from 550.
September 5. Le Havre. Helped the army out. The place was pranged good and proper. Not much flak.
September 8. Le Havre. No joy. 10/10. Abandoned. Our kite is 'V'. George brought her in. Burst a tyre. Bogged. Cor!
September 10. Le Havre. No flak. Very easy trip.
September 12. Frankfurt. Bloody awful trip. Good prang though. Bags of twitch.

first to become truly operational, flying a 'second dickey' trip as a co-pilot to a more experienced skipper on 26 August to give him a foretaste of what was to come. Five nights later the crew took part in their first operation together; it was very nearly their last.

Peter's diary summarized the raid as follows: 'Operation – Stettin. Almost didn't come back. Attacked twice. Bang on bombing. 9.05 hrs. Outside loop in kite. Good photo. 1 x 4,000lb. 48 x 30lb. 500 x 4lb.'

They had indeed come very close to being shot down. At 0232 hours and at a height of 10,000 feet on the homeward leg, 'Mac' Macnamara in the rear turret spotted a Messerschmitt Bf110 on the starboard quarter above, just at the point that it opened fire from 350 yards range. 'Mac' returned fire,

The operation on 8 September may have had more serious consequences for the crew. Landing an aircraft with its bombs still on board was obviously more dangerous than when it was empty and, as George eased the heavy bomber down onto the tarmac, a tyre exploded, causing the aircraft to swing violently. In what was later described in the Squadron Operations Record Book (ORB) as 'a spectacular and skilful landing', George managed to keep the aircraft straight, gradually reducing speed until the final moment when the Lancaster suddenly swung to starboard and slewed 180 degrees until it was facing the wrong way up the runway.

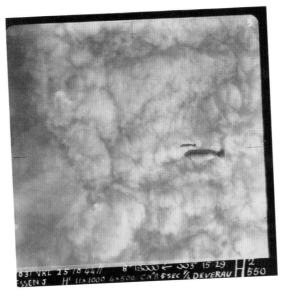

Right Bombing
photograph, Essen,
25 October 1944.
(Sean Feast)

Even after only a handful of ops, the crew had come to the attention of the new commanding officer, Wing Commander 'Dinger' Bell. Bell, as with all squadron commanders, was obliged to provide a quota of crews for training as Pathfinders – the corps elite of Bomber Command. After their return from Frankfurt, George was told that the crew would be posted to Pathfinder Navigation Training Unit (NTU), but for some reason their posting was cancelled. Peter was disappointed: 'Posting cancelled,' he wrote. 'They want a more experienced crew. Lay in bed all afternoon feeling sorry for myself.'

The strain of operations was already beginning to tell, and manifested itself in a series of niggling arguments between Peter and the navigator, William Cross. On 16 September, Peter reported sick, and the crew flew without him, returning safely. Four nights later, Peter was himself the 'spare bod' in Flight Sergeant Hopman's crew for an attack on troop concentrations near Calais. He returned to the good news that his 'crown' had come through – an elevation in rank to flight sergeant, evidenced by a silver crown sitting atop the sergeant's chevrons.

Trips to Neuss (23 September) and Calais (28 September) followed, until the crew was given leave. Rather than going immediately home to Mitcham, Peter instead headed first for Manchester, and the home of the new love of his life, Kathleen. 'Kit', as she was known, had been a feature of Peter's life since the early spring, with regular musings in his diary as to his feelings towards her,

and his delight at the good impression she had made upon meeting his father.

Returning from leave, Peter and the crew embarked on a busy period of operations, including two trips to Duisberg (on 14 and 15 October), one to Stuttgart (20 October) and two to Essen (23 and 25 October, the latter with a 'second dickey'). Three more trips were flown before the month was out, including a daylight trip to Cologne (16 October) and a further daylight one to Walcheren (29 October) – a trip for which they were specially selected and achieved 'a good prang'.

Writing to his father on 29 October, Peter spoke of the contrast between the dangers of operations and the safety of the Mess: 'Ours is a peculiar existence. At one hour we are living in a fairly quiet and friendly atmosphere of the mess – and in a few hours we are plunged into a ghastly holocaust which makes the blitz on London look like a kid's game – Cologne, Duisberg, Essen – those towns just don't exist any more.'

The first week of November comprised a successful sortie to Düsseldorf and an equally unsuccessful trip to Bochum. Now with their own aircraft, they decided to give it a name and settled upon 'Bouncing Baby'. Its first outing was to Gelsenkirchen for a daylight raid that was flown in formation. Peter describes the experience simply as 'horrible'. One of their number, Flying Officer Leonard McCarthy, failed to return. Peter was a good friend of one of the crew:

So far we have not finished ops [Peter wrote the next day]. We have done quite a few lately – five in nine days – and are now on the last third of the tour. On Gelsenkirchen on Monday, we stopped quite a few bits of metal but none of us was hurt. On that trip I lost one of my best pals, a chap named Colbourne, an air bomber and all of his crew. He was one of the best fellows I have ever met and when we learned that he had been posted missing I felt just bloody awful but, as one wit said, 'that's what we're paid for'.

With twenty-one operations completed, Peter was clearly impatient to finish his tour. His patience was tested further when, on 7 November, they were

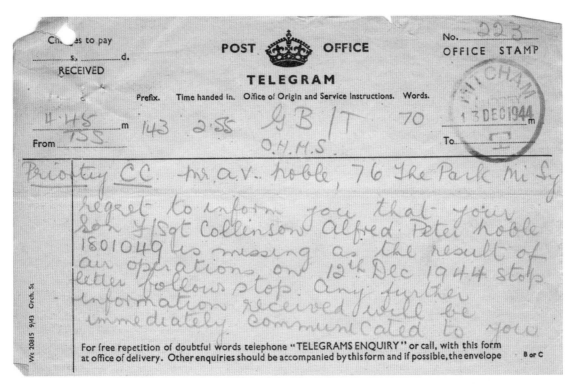

Left
Missing telegram sent
to Peter's father by
the OC No. 150
Squadron. *(Sean Feast)*

Left Peter kept a note
of every operation in
his diary. Poignantly,
the final entry ends
with his 23rd trip.
(Sean Feast)

Right The original
wooden cross that
marked Peter's grave.
(Via Sean Feast)

Right Author Sean
Feast at the grave of
his Great Uncle Peter
Noble, Reichswald
Forest War Cemetery.
(Sean Feast)

posted to RAF Fiskerton in preparation for moving to RAF Hemswell. The reason was that C Flight was being hived off to form the nucleus of a new unit – No. 150 Squadron – but Hemswell was not quite ready for their arrival. Peter described Fiskerton as 'a horrible dump', but his mood was improved when he learned that the new officer commanding was Wing Commander Glen Avis, who had been his flight commander at RAF Wymeswold, and that the bombing leader was similarly ex-28 OTU. 'Most of the ground crew have never worked on Lancs before,' he noted, with more than a hint of irony.

By now, the Devereau crew was the most senior on the Squadron, and Peter was the senior air bomber. His high standard of bombing was being maintained and actually achieved national recognition when one of his bombing photographs appeared – uncredited of course – in the November issue of *The Aeroplane*: 'On Friday we helped the army out a bit,' he wrote. 'The boys and I felt very self-satisfied when we saw a bombing photo of ours had been published in *The Aeroplane*. The picture was of the Hohenzollen bridge – or rather the remains thereof – at Cologne.'

Two trips were flown from Fiskerton: one to Düren, which Peter described as 'accurate', and the second to Wanne-Eickel, where he dropped one 4,000lb and sixteen 500lb bombs for 'a nice prang'. It is his last diary entry.

On 5 December, Peter wrote a final letter to his father. In it he reassures his father that recent trips have been 'uneventful' and that, when the target is obscured by cloud, he is obliged to drop his bombs on ETA: 'We probably killed some German cows or something,' he says. Exactly a week later, Peter's aircraft received a direct hit from a heavy flak shell, and burst into flames. It crashed in the target area, killing everyone on board. Six bodies were identified, and buried in a cemetery local to Essen. The seventh – that of Bill Horlor – was never recovered.

Wing Commander Avis, in his letter to Peter's father, described him as having a cheerful personality: 'He will be greatly missed both in the Squadron and amongst his fellow NCOs in the sergeants' mess where he had many friends. He was a very popular NCO and has proved himself to be an excellent air bomber who could always be relied upon by all other members of his crew.'

Although his death was presumed for official purposes as from 12 December 1944, it was actually four years later that the RAF Missing Research and Enquiry Service in Germany located his place of burial. Originally buried in Essen South Western Cemetery, Peter and the five others whose bodies had been found were reinterred at the new British military cemetery in the Reichswald Forest on the Dutch/German border.

His father added an inscription to the base of

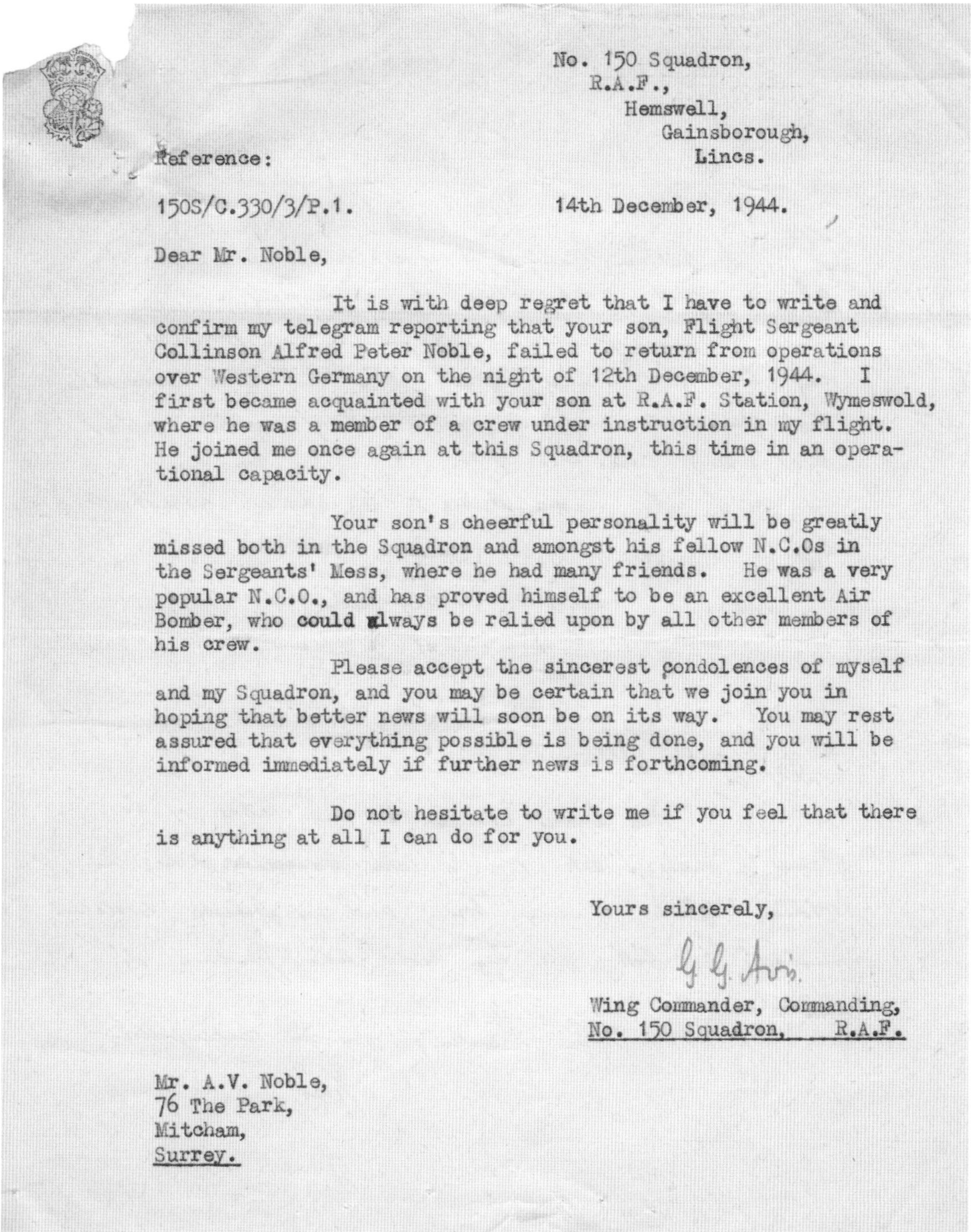

No. 150 Squadron,
R.A.F.,
Hemswell,
Gainsborough,
Lincs.

Reference:

150S/C.330/3/P.1.   14th December, 1944.

Dear Mr. Noble,

      It is with deep regret that I have to write and
confirm my telegram reporting that your son, Flight Sergeant
Collinson Alfred Peter Noble, failed to return from operations
over Western Germany on the night of 12th December, 1944.   I
first became acquainted with your son at R.A.F. Station, Wymeswold,
where he was a member of a crew under instruction in my flight.
He joined me once again at this Squadron, this time in an operational capacity.

      Your son's cheerful personality will be greatly
missed both in the Squadron and amongst his fellow N.C.Os in
the Sergeants' Mess, where he had many friends.   He was a very
popular N.C.O., and has proved himself to be an excellent Air
Bomber, who **could** always be relied upon by all other members of
his crew.

      Please accept the sincerest condolences of myself
and my Squadron, and you may be certain that we join you in
hoping that better news will soon be on its way.   You may rest
assured that everything possible is being done, and you will be
informed immediately if further news is forthcoming.

      Do not hesitate to write me if you feel that there
is anything at all I can do for you.

Yours sincerely,

G G Avis.

Wing Commander, Commanding,
No. 150 Squadron,   R.A.F.

Mr. A.V. Noble,
76 The Park,
Mitcham,
Surrey.

Left Official
confirmation of
Peter's death was not
received by the family
until three years after
the war had ended.
(Via Sean Feast)

the headstone, a few lines taken from the Gettys-
burg Address: 'The last full measure of his devotion.'
In the visitors' book, the simple sentence had been
added: 'They gave their lives, so that we may live in
peace.'

In a letter to Peter's father from Kit's family, he
was described with clear fondness: 'He was boist-
erous, he came in like a gust of wind but we would
not have had him to be otherwise. It was his trade-
mark – open and frank as the open spaces. Loveable,
generous and always cheerful.'

This was the man in the photograph on my grandfather's office wall. ●

CHAPTER ELEVEN

THE LONG VOYAGE TO WAR

SEAN FEAST

AS THE STORM CLOUDS GATHERED IN NORTHERN EUROPE IN THE LATE SUMMER OF 1939, JACK TOOTAL WAS NEARLY 6,000 MILES AWAY IN THE SUNSHINE OF RIO DE JANEIRO, AT THE OFFICES OF THE BANK OF LONDON AND SOUTH AMERICA LTD. WHEN JACK HAD LEFT HIS HOME IN THE GARDEN OF ENGLAND FOR THE ADVENTURES OF SOUTH AMERICA, HE COULD NOT POSSIBLY HAVE KNOWN HOW EVENTS WOULD UNFOLD. HE SHOULD HAVE BEEN HAPPY, FOR HE HAD ONLY RECENTLY MET THE LOVE OF HIS LIFE AND WAS KEEN TO TELL HIS PARENTS THE GOOD NEWS. BUT INSTEAD HE WAS WORRIED – WAITING FOR WAR TO BE DECLARED AND ANXIOUS TO BE HOME.

ORN ON 17 MAY 1918 as one of four children, Jack Tootal became an inveterate letter-writer almost as soon as he could pick up a pen, and it is through these letters that we are able not only to track his physical movements throughout the war, but also to gain a deeper insight into his personal thoughts – his struggle with being distant from his loved ones for prolonged periods overseas and his desire to see action and 'do his bit' for king and country.

Even at prep school, Jack's spirit of determination shines through in his writing, as he resolutely disregards any feelings of homesickness and focuses instead on practical necessities such as the need for more books, more sweets and his fishing rod! On leaving Sevenoaks School in the summer of 1936, he considered his career prospects. His father – a senior banking official in Lisbon at the time – had the answer; he engineered a place for his son at the Bank of London and South America, initially at head office. Having served his apprenticeship, Jack volunteered for services overseas, and on 27 January 1939 set sail for Rio on the *Highland Chieftain*.

From his arrival in February of that year, Jack's life, for a few short happy months at least, was quite literally – and metaphorically – a carnival. South America was the destination for many hundreds of young men in the 1930s as they sought adventure and reward in a land that was thousands of miles geographically and million of miles culturally from their own country. Jack's father had worked there, and one of his older brothers, Stanley, was currently there, working for a flourmill in Sao Paulo.

Through the bank, Jack began seeing a beautiful 19-year-old secretary called Geraldine – although she was always referred to as 'Deenie' – and he was quickly besotted and equally quickly engaged – at first unofficially. As if sensing the possibility of his own parents' disapproval, Jack wrote to them on the eve of war (2 September 1939), describing Deenie as 'Mr and Mrs Rogers' favourite daughter' whom he had unofficially asked to marry him: 'Rogers are OK about it if the Toots' family is,' he wrote. 'Send me a cable with "Yes!"'

The long weeks waiting for a reply were an obvious strain. Jack wrote to his parents again on 7 October expressing concern that he had not heard from them since 17 August and reassuring them that his love 'is not just a passing affair – we really are earnest'. When his parents did finally reply, Jack clearly received the response he was hoping for, and was pleased with their encouraging words. He replied: 'She is one of the sweetest and most wonderful girls in the world and I don't think I could live without her.' As for becoming officially engaged, however, they hit upon a snag; the bank would not allow it: 'I only wish the bank was more human,' he moaned.

Jack's immediate thought was to return home, but he was dissuaded from doing so by his father,

Left Jack as a schoolboy. Fishing rods were as important as school books! *(Tootal family)*

who countenanced caution. While his family was already on a war footing, Jack was told to stay put, and not jeopardize either his contract, or his father's guarantee! It was a difficult time, waiting, made more difficult still with the knowledge that another of his brothers, Cecil, a pilot in the Royal Air Force, was already in the thick of the action. Jack's spare time, on the other hand, was given over to supporting the Red Cross.

Right
Flight Lieutenant Jack
Tootal. *(Tootal family)*

It was not until the late autumn of 1940, after Jack and Deenie had been married in the September at the Anglican Church in Rio, that the two of them at last secured a passage home, reputedly sailing as part of Convoy HX84, which set sail on 28 October. Comprising some thirty-eight ships, the convoy was intercepted by the German heavy cruiser *Admiral Scheer*, which caused all the ships to scatter. Happily, they made it home, although

been further elevated in the ranks to temporary sergeant. He completed his training at No. 2 School of Air Navigation, almost exactly a year after he had enlisted, and shortly after his son Patrick was born.

Jack's talent as a pilot, and his calm authority in the air, had been remarked upon by his superiors. Rather than receive the operational posting that he no doubt desired, Jack was instead held back as an instructor. He was posted to No. 3 SFTS, RAF

Left With his new wife at his side, Jack prepares to set sail for home after his South American adventure. *(Tootal family)*

their sole escort – HMS *Jervis Bay* – was sunk in a heroic action that earned her captain the Victoria Cross.

He finally stepped ashore in November 1940, with a pregnant Deenie at his side. Within weeks Jack had enlisted as an aircraftman 2nd class/ aircrafthand/pilot in the Royal Air Force Volunteer Reserve and soon after began training at No. 4 Initial Training Wing (ITW). With his obligatory square bashing completed, and a promotion to leading aircraftman (LAC), Jack began his pilot training at No. 8 Elementary Flying Training School (EFTS) and then at No. 14 Service Flying Training School (SFTS), by which time he had

South Cerney, where he would remain for ten months, instructing a succession of fledgling pilots into the intricacies of flying larger aircraft, the unit having become a Group II school specializing in twin-engine training using the Airspeed Oxford.

Instructing, although essential, could be frustrating for those keen to get on 'ops', but Jack's Air Force career seemed destined to follow a particular path. He had some consolation in the February of 1942 when he was formally discharged on appointment to a commission, and was thus able to put up his first 'ring' – albeit a thin one – as a pilot officer on probation. For a brief few weeks, Jack was posted to No. 3 School of General Reconnaissance, during which time he wrote to his parents and appears resigned to a life on the fringes of combat: 'I have put in an application to go to Brazil,' he wrote, 'as some sort of liaison for the RAF, and shot them a line about knowing the language and had influential friends.' His application came to nothing, but, not long after being promoted to flying officer in October 1942, he found himself in Blackpool, with the days dragging slowly by as he awaited a ship to take him to India.

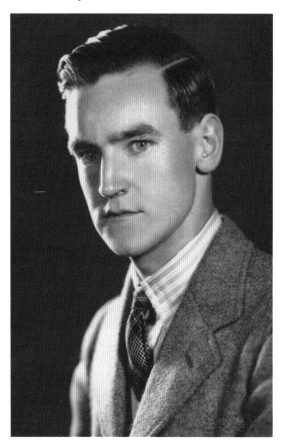

Right A formal portrait of Jack Tootal, prior to joining the RAF *(Tootal family)*

By now a seasoned traveller and with experience of long voyages, Jack compared his journey to the sub-continent as being, in part, 'like a pleasure cruise', with the exception of 'the overcrowding and bags of lifeboat drill'. As the weeks roll slowly by, and with stopovers at Durban (South Africa) and Diego Suarey (Madagascar), his initial enthusiasm is tempered by a weary acceptance of military routine: 'This voyage never seems to end but conditions are pretty good. I am troop deck officer and I have to look after about 200 men – it is hard work but the men appreciate it.'

His aerograms during this period are not dated, or else the dates and location have been removed by the sensor, but by the early spring of 1943 Jack has at last arrived at Air HQ, India, and is beginning to find his feet: 'It is nice being able to get unpacked and not live in trunks,' he writes. 'I have moved into a nice single officers' quarters, which consists of a bed, sitting room, dressing room and a bathroom. You have to furnish it yourself but you can hire furniture fairly cheaply and you can make it very comfortable. Aircrew do fairly well for leave,' he continues. '[We can] expect a fortnight in the hills to escape the oppressive heat.'

His excitement at being in India comes through in his writing, and his somewhat 'soft' landing is helped by the fact that his previous 'boss' at South Cerney is there to greet him upon arrival: 'I met my old boss from South Cerney – he is the navigation officer to the Group [and] an awfully nice chap.' This same letter home (dated 14 March 1943) contains details of his daily existence as an instructor at 1 SFTS, and the problems he immediately encounters with the high cost of living, despite being paid a better wage: 'I have a manservant called a "bearer" – he does everything – brings me a cup of tea, puts out the clothes I am going to wear – waits on me at table and a hundred other things.' He continued 'There are two cinemas, 'but the films are very old ones. I have given up drinking as it is too expensive; cigarettes, thank goodness, are still fairly cheap!'

Within days of his arrival, however, Jack was struck down with jaundice, and immediately hospitalized, bemoaning that he was 'yellow all over'. Laid up for over a week, he admits to being more than a little weary at the point that he resumes duties – duties, he remarks, that are very similar to those he carried out in the UK, but adapted to the local environment and the intense heat that preceded the monsoon: 'I get up at 5.30 and have breakfast at 9.00. I work until 2.30 and then have lunch. I then sleep until 6.00pm. My days are very full,' he added, 'and I am doing the work of a squadron leader.'

The deadly dull routine, the absence from his loved ones and the realization that he was only a few short months into a posting that might potentially last anything up to three years began to

Left Father and son: with young Patrick on his knee. *(Tootal family)*

Despite these occasional distractions, Jack seemed further away from the 'real' war than ever, and was keen to hear news of his brother Cecil, who had by now been promoted to wing commander and successfully completed Staff College. On 14 August 1943 he wrote, perhaps more in hope than any real expectation: 'I may not have to do three years out here after all.'

In the event, he was right, but it was still another eight months before he saw England again, sending a telegram to his parents on 25 April 1944 to say that he had arrived safe and well.

take its toll. A promotion to flight lieutenant (acting) in July 1943 proved a welcome fillip, providing him with more money and quarters closer to the Mess. The tedium of service life was occasionally enlivened by a game of bridge or an even more occasional dance, although Jack admits to spending much of the time on the sidelines, watching the others: 'There is always a shortage of women...' He even had the dubious honour of defending an airman in a court martial. Although the details or indeed the outcome are not known, Jack says that 'by all accounts I did quite well'. One assumes on that basis that the airman got off lightly!

There was a short period of leave with his wife and young son Patrick, but the Royal Air Force was quick to put Jack back into the training regime, but this time with the boot on the other foot, for Jack returned to RAF South Cerney for an Advanced Flying Course. The irony was not lost on him: 'It will be funny going back to be instructed where I instructed,' he wrote.

While training, Jack decided he would try and pull a few strings and use his brother's influence to secure him a posting. Whatever the brothers were plotting between them, it did not come off, Jack

Left One of the family album: Jack, 'Deenie' and Patrick. *(Tootal family)*

Jack (seated third from right) as a flight lieutenant with fellow officers and NCOs at Air HQ, India. *(Tootal family)*

observing in a letter dated 1 August 1944: 'What I
asked Cecil for has not come off... not in Cecil's
Command.'

From No. 3 (Pilot) Advanced Flying Unit Jack
was posted to No. 83 Operational Training Unit
(OTU) at RAF Peplow to be prepared for operations, but for many weeks he did not even sit in the
cockpit of an aircraft, let alone fly one. When at
last his operational training began in earnest, it was
over almost as soon as it had started; indeed, it must
have been amusing for the instructors to compare
notes with their pupil over how many flying hours
they had logged between them! Posted again to
RAF Riccall in Yorkshire (41 Base) at the end of
October 1944, he again patiently bided his time
over Christmas, where the highlight proved to be
the officers serving the airmen their Christmas
turkey, and his constant foraging for cigars for his
father.

On 31 January 1945, after a train journey lasting
more than two days, he finally arrived at his
operational station, RAF Foulsham, and reported
to Wing Commander Peter Paull DFC, the officer
commanding No. 462 Squadron, Royal Australian
Air Force (RAAF).

Jack had struck lucky with No. 462 Squadron. The
unit, until recently under the command of the
famous Australian 'Dambuster' Wing Commander
David Shannon DFC, had not been much impressed when it had been pulled off bomber
operations with No. 4 Group to transfer to No. 100
Group (Bomber Support).

Now, as well as the occasional bomb, they would
also drop thousands of strips of metal foil –
Window – in order to disrupt German radar. Later
they would also carry an extra crewman to operate
sophisticated radio counter measures (RCM)
equipment, all with the singular purpose of spoofing the Germans and protecting the bomber
streams against nightfighter attack.

To carry its specialist equipment, the Squadron
was equipped with adapted Handley Page Halifax
Mk IIIs, instantly recognizable as 'special' aircraft
because of the enormous aerials that protruded
from their bodies, and the automatic 'Window'
layer that sat aft of the H2S radar 'dome'.

Reliability was occasionally an issue, however. On
the night of 7/8 February, for example, an engine
fire soon after take-off obliged one of the Squadron's pilots to order his crew to bale out, which they
did successfully. He then skilfully crash-landed the
aircraft at nearby Hethel (today the home to Lotus
Cars) without further incident.

Jack had his own excitement to contend with on
the early evening of 18 February. Having attended
the briefing for operations, and no doubt with the
adrenalin pumping at the thought of his first
operation, his curtain-raiser proved to be something of a disappointing dress rehearsal when a tyre
burst while he was taxying to take-off. Although the
ground crews were quick to respond, it was not
possible to get a new tyre fitted in time and Jack's
operation was therefore scrubbed.

He had more luck, however, on the night of
20/21 February. He had spent some of the day
penning a letter to his parents. Although the harsh
winter had forced many operations to be cancelled,
it had given him time to settle in and learn the
ropes. It had also allowed him time to get to know
his Squadron contemporaries. His opinion of them
was especially warm, and their opinion of him was
similarly welcoming: 'I have made some good
friends here and the whole Squadron seems very
friendly and all out to help one,' he wrote. 'I am
eating much better and should put on weight again.
I may get leave again about the end of March but
cannot be sure.'

That night he flew on ops for the first time. A
clear sunny day had been followed by an equally
clear and cloudless night. A maximum effort of
fourteen aircraft was required, and all of the
aircraft – including Halifax PN429 flown by Flight
Lieutenant J. S. Tootal with seven crew – got away
safely shortly after 2200 hours. The operation was
typical for the time: a special duties flight to
Heilbronn, a 'spoof' to confuse the enemy defences
and to draw the nightfighters away from the Main
Force attack on Dortmund. As well as 'Window' to
play havoc with the German radar, the Squadron
aircraft also carried bombs – in Jack's case four
general purpose (GP) 500-pounders to add further
authenticity to the deception. Jack landed safely at
0431 hours after a trip of a little under six and a
half hours.

No. 462 (RAAF) Squadron,
Royal Air Force,
FOULSHAM,
Norfolk.

462S/C.1714/14/P1.   26th February, 1945.

Dear *Mr. Tootal*.

    It is my unhappy task to confirm the news that you will have
already received that your Son, Flight Lieutenant John Stewart Tootal,
was reported missing from an operational flight from this country
on the night of 24th February, 1945.

    I would like to express my heartfelt sympathy and deep regret
at this anxious time. Your Son will be missed very greatly by the
members of this Squadron, the attitude of determination and
resolution adopted by him and his crew have made a profound impression
here, and their efficiency and gallantry will long be remembered.

    The most searching enquiries have been made through every
channel but have so far revealed nothing. Meanwhile we can only
hope that your Son and the other members of his crew are either in
safe hands or are prisoners of war.

    It is desired to explain that the request in the telegram
notifying you that your Son was a casualty, was included with the
object of avoiding his chance of escape being prejudiced by undue
publicity in case he was still at large. This is not to say that
any information about him is available, but is a precaution adopted
in the case of all personnel reported missing.

    Once again, may I convey to you my deepest sympathy and the
hope that I may be able to convey to you happier news at a later date.

            Yours *Very Sincerely*

C. Jackson

(C. W. JACKSON) S/Ldr.,
462 Squadron, FOULSHAM.

E. A. Tootal, Esq.,
"Casanova",
Sevenoaks, Kent.

The bodies of Jack and his crew being reburied with full military honours, November 1945.

Right The official
Air Ministry letter
that confirms Jack's
death and place of
burial *(Tootal family)*

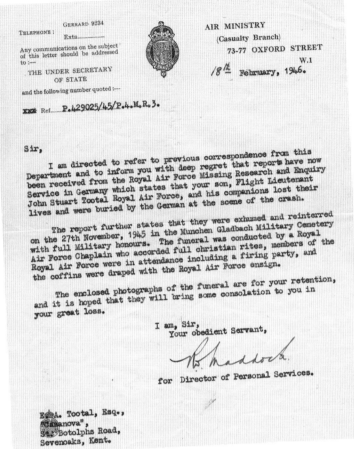

TELEPHONE : GERRARD 9234
Extn...............

Any communications on the subject
of this letter should be addressed
to :—
THE UNDER SECRETARY
OF STATE

and the following number quoted :—

Ref. P.429025/45/P.4.M.R.3.

AIR MINISTRY
(Casualty Branch)
73-77 OXFORD STREET
W.1

18th February, 1946.

Sir,

I am directed to refer to previous correspondence from this Department and to inform you with deep regret that reports have now been received from the Royal Air Force Missing Research and Enquiry Service in Germany which states that your son, Flight Lieutenant John Stuart Tootal Royal Air Force, and his companions lost their lives and were buried by the German at the scene of the crash.

The report further states that they were exhumed and reinterred on the 27th November, 1945 in the Munchen Gladbach Military Cemetery with full Military honours. The funeral was conducted by a Royal Air Force Chaplain who accorded full christian rites, members of the Royal Air Force were in attendance including a firing party, and the coffins were draped with the Royal Air Force ensign.

The enclosed photographs of the funeral are for your retention, and it is hoped that they will bring some consolation to you in your great loss.

I am, Sir,
Your obedient Servant,

for Director of Personal Services.

E.A. Tootal, Esq.,
"Casanova",
St. Botolphs Road,
Sevenoaks, Kent.

He flew again on the 22nd, taking off shortly before 1800 hours – one of the last to get away. He was flying Halifax MZ370. On this occasion it was a 'spoof' to the Ruhr involving eight aircraft. All took off and returned safely.

On 24 February, after a busy few days for the Squadron and for Jack, ten aircraft were detailed for night operations. It was planned as a 'spoof' for an attack on Neuss, joining a number of aircraft from the training establishments on a diversionary, with take-off scheduled for 1700 hours and a return by 2150 hours. In what was to prove a disastrous night for 462, only six of the ten aircraft returned. Among the missing were Flight Lieutenant Jack Tootal and crew.

Jack had taken off in good weather at 1703 hours – one of the first to get away. His crew comprised two other Englishmen (Sergeant Trevor David, flight engineer, and Flight Sergeant Geoffrey Harrison-Broadley, the specialist equipment officer) and five Australians (Flight Sergeant William

Duncan, navigator; Warrant Officer Ernest Oliver, the air bomber; Warrant Officer Norman Hall, the wireless op; Flight Sergeant Patrick Carlon, the mid-upper gunner; and Flight Sergeant Murray Smith, the rear gunner).

The first Squadron aircraft to return began landing shortly after 2200 hours. By the early hours of 25 February, it was clear that four aircraft were now overdue. Unless they had landed elsewhere – and as yet there had been no reports to that effect – the news could only be bad. There was a palpable sense of disbelief within the Squadron as ground crews waited at dispersal for aircraft and men that would never return. Against four captains of aircraft – Flight Lieutenant Jack Tootal, Flight Lieutenant Allan Rate, Flight Lieutenant Frederick Ridgewell and Flying Officer Vivian Ely – the Squadron adjutant marked the Operations Record Book (ORB) in the 'details of sorties or flight' column with the familiar term: 'failed to return'.

All four, it transpired, had been shot down by nightfighters on leaving the target area: Vivian Ely, a 23-year-old Australian, was shot down by Oberfeldwebel Walter Kreibaum of III./NJG11 for his first 'kill'. There were no survivors, and Kreibaum was himself obliged to take to his parachute shortly afterwards on account of an engine fire. Of the other three that were lost, Jack's aircraft (PN429) came down at Munchengladbach, while Allan Rate (MZ447) and Frederick Ridgewell (MZ448) both crashed to the south-east of Breyell. Ridgewell's aircraft was hit at 15,000 feet, a few minutes after it had dropped its load of incendiaries. With a hit in the overload fuel tanks, the skipper just had time to order his crew to bale out before the Halifax exploded. Four of his crew made it out. Only one of the crew escaped from Allan Rate's aircraft, Flight Sergeant Reg Gould, and he had the horror of watching his Halifax fall to earth close to the blazing wreck of Ridgewell's aircraft.

Besides Kreibaum, three German pilots made claims for victories that coincide precisely with these losses: Hauptmann Josef Kraft of 12./NJG1, Major Max Eckhoff of Stab II./NJG2 and Oberleutnant Heinz Reuter of 12./NJG3. All three were 'aces', Kraft with forty-nine 'kills' to his name.

Within hours the obligatory telegram arrived at Jack's parents in Sevenoaks, followed by a letter on behalf of the Squadron CO. Long days stretched into weeks as the family – and indeed the Squadron – awaited news. None came. Wing Commander Paull wrote to Jack's brother, Cecil, on 15 March:

We have absolutely no information as to what happened [the letter says], but apparently the Squadron were [sic] intercepted as unfortunately the aircraft of which your brother was captain was not our only loss that night. I am very sorry I cannot give you any information as to the type of work the Squadron was doing that night; I take it that you know [he] was the captain of a heavy bomber type aircraft.

I would like to assure you [it continues], that 'Toots' was held in the highest esteem by us all and on a previous operation had shown his good value to us all. He seemed extremely keen to 'press on' and his popularity was rather unusual considering the short time he had been with us.

Paull still held out hope that Jack might yet turn up alive: 'The hun, as recently as last night, claimed to have just taken prisoner one of our chaps lost on the same night... it shows us what excellent hope there is of others turning up.'

Sadly, it was not to be. Paull wrote again, to Jack's sister Marjorie, in October 1945, as he was waiting for his berth on a ship to take him home: 'There are two crews about which we have had no news,' he writes, 'which is most disappointing. Our squadron has been disbanded for about a month now and so of course no official news would come to me any more...'

It would be another nine months before Jack's death was finally confirmed in an official letter from the RAF Missing Research and Enquiry Service. Originally buried by the Germans close to where his aircraft came down, he now rests with his crew in the Rheinberg War Cemetery in Germany. ●

Left The original cross marking Jack's grave. *(Tootal family)*

Left Jack Tootal and his crew are buried alongside one another in the same cemetery at Rheinberg. Jack's grave is identified by the blue wreath. *(Tootal family)*

ACKNOWLEDGEMENTS AND NOTES

Chapter One (Julian Evan-Hart)
With special thanks to Edwin van Engelen and his colleagues Chris de Boer, Richard de Mos and Erwin Rust; to Forester Erik van Barneveld, who is responsible for the area of Woudschoten/Zeist; to Rob van den Nieuwendijk, a researcher whose earlier work was consulted; to H. Wilson; to Raimondo Bogaars; to the Internet Forum website 12 O'Clock High and its members Doug Stankey and Chris Goss; to the Luftwaffe Experten Message Board; and, in particular, to the efforts of Peter D. Evans.

Chapter Two (Steve Darlow)
With special thanks to Linzee Druce, who helped with the story of Jock's initial evasion in Norway. See www.archieraf.co.uk for further details of the evasion and also the story of her grandfather, William Archibald, who was lost on 30/31 March 1942 raid on the *Tirpitz*. Thanks also extend to

Kevin and Lynn Defty. Jock Morrison passed away in 2012.

Chapter Three (Linzee Druce)
My grateful thanks to Andy Brown and for his perseverance in ensuring the crew of Wellington R1646 will be remembered. I am indebted to relatives of the airmen from Wellington R1646 for their assistance and contributions from their family archives: Joan Felt, Marjorie Columbus, Alan Thomson, Margaret Thomson, Betti Murray (Thomson), Mary-Lynn Dodson, Erik Ryalen, Joan Graham (Jackson), John Fritz, Harry Kelley (Kelley), Robert Bateson, Christine Townsend (Riley), Bob and Rae Fell, Graham Milliken, Lizzie Murphy (Milliken), Colin and Eric Greenbank, Paul and Christopher Greenbank (Greenbank). In addition, thanks to Steve 'Smudger' Smith for help with 218 Squadron information, to Colin McKenzie and Keith Bryers

for details from their archives, and, finally, a very special thanks to Morten Moe for his help and support.

Chapter Four (Julian Evan-Hart)
With thanks to Cynrik De Decker and Wim Govaerts.

Chapter Five (Steve Bond)
After the war Les stayed on in the RAF as a flight engineer until 1965 when he joined Monarch Airlines, finally retiring in 1981 with 17,000 hours in his logbook. He lived in Wing, Buckingham-shire and became a stalwart of the local branch of the Aircrew Association. Always generous with his time and ready to recount a host of anecdotes, Les sadly died in 2008.

Chapter Six (Steve Bond)
Richard flew post-war for two more years with No. 242 Squadron Transport Command on Stirlings, and then Yorks before he decided to leave to support his widowed mother and returned to his home town of Liverpool. Both he and his son Steve were of tremendous help in putting his story together for which I thank them both.

Chapter Seven (Sean Feast)
I would very much like to thank Rita, David, Tracey and Simon Fisher for their help, and especially Richard Fisher for acting as the conduit to introduce me to his lovely family. I hope between us we have done Harry proud.

Chapter Eight (Steve Darlow)
A special thank you to Henry Oakeby for his recollections, although it is with regret that we were not able to publish his story before he passed away.

Chapter Nine (Andrew Macdonald)
I would like to thank the following people for their assistance with this article: Mr Graham Clarke – cousin of Howard Cornish, Mr Howard Wigg – son of Terry Wigg, Mr Mervyn Pask – former wireless operator/air gunner, Nos 625 and 617 Squadrons RAF, Mr Robert Pattison DFC – No. 625 Squadron RAF, Mr Kenneth Johnson –

former air gunner – Nos 9 and 61 Squadrons RAF, Mr Dennis Over – former air gunner Nos 106 and 227 Squadrons RAF, Mr Nic Lewis – Honorary Secretary of the No. 625 Squadron RAF Memorial Association.

Chapter Ten (Sean Feast)
This was an emotional project (I hesitate to say 'journey'!) more than 40 years in the making. I would like to thank Peter's late brother, Bill, for leaving me a great treasure trove of memories, letters and photographs that enabled me to understand more about my Great Uncle and indeed the whole Noble family. To Shirley, Mary and Petra Noble a huge thank you; to my mum June (née Noble) the biggest thanks of all, for this was her quest as much as mine.

Chapter Eleven (Sean Feast)
I am indebted to Jack's son Patrick (Group Captain Patrick Tootal OBE, DL) for his help in preparing the chapter on his father, and answering my frequent questions to ensure that Jack's contribution to the war effort – and the thousands of others who provided such essential training support – was properly recorded. Jack's grandson is Colonel Stuart Tootal DSO, OBE – late 3 Para and Commander of the first Battle Group in Helmand. Although Stuart never knew his grandfather, he is proud of Jack's sacrifice. I would also like to thank Jamie Hibberd for giving me a steer on 462 Squadron through the Australian archive.

INDEX